ABSENT WITNESS

ABSENT WITNESS

Karl Petry

With Karen McLean

Visionary Living, Inc.
New Milford, Connecticut

Absent Witness

By Karl Petry
With Karen McLean

Cover photo of Karl Petry by Matthew Pasterchick
Cover and interior design by Leslie McAllister
Editor: Rosemary Ellen Guiley

ISBN: 978-1-942157-04-5 (pbk)
ISBN: 978-1-942157-05-2 (e-pub)

Published by Visionary Living, Inc.
New Milford, Connecticut
www.visionaryliving.com

Table of Contents

Foreword
by Paula Roberts

I met Karl in the winter of 1997 at the first of what was supposed to be a regular meeting of people with an interest in parapsychology. As soon as we saw each other we recognized a kindred spirit and, indeed, we were the only people there with "the gift." Karl and I became better acquainted over the years that followed.

I describe Karl to others by asking, "Have you seen *The Sixth Sense*?" This is the best way I know to give anyone a small idea of Karl's extraordinary gifts. He is a phenomenon—I know of no one else in my many years in this field who constantly lives in a "time-slip" and can also have meaningful communication with spirits of the dead about issues concerning their lives or their relatives. Certainly, there are others who also have this ability, but no one I have ever heard of does this all the time like Karl. While carrying on a normal conversation, Karl can also be observing walls melting away or with different decoration, and sometimes see earlier residents going about their daily lives.

For example, one warm summer evening, Karl was driving me back to Manhattan from New Jersey when he suddenly announced, "It is snowing!" This struck me as a bizarre comment. He went on to describe cars of another era driving around us as we went through Central Park. I realized he was in a time slip, seeing New York City in another time, as though it were happening in the present.

Karl also has the ability to see great detail in his visions. In my apartment block where I live, I have long corridors in which I have often seen apparitional forms that look like smoky shadows. When Karl sees them, they are not just shadows, but people, such as a woman in a hat checking her stocking seams.

These examples are just the tip of the iceberg of what Karl is capable of perceiving, as you will discover in his amazing cases in this book.

When I first met Karl, he had yet to acknowledge his gift publicly. I know from my own path how difficult that can be in the face of the skepticism of others. In my case, it came from families with deep roots in the Catholic faith, which does not embrace our field at all. I feel Karl in his way, and I in mine, are ambassadors for the paranormal. I frequently say to people, "I may look normal, but I am certainly not." We are putting a reasonable face upon something that scares many people. Too many times to count, have I seen "the shutters" come down on people's faces when I tell them what I do, so it is a pleasure to have someone with whom I can share these experiences and also work with on haunted locations. Most important of all, and quite unique in my view of this field, we are totally without jealousy of each other. We respect our similarities and our differences.

In 2001 both Karl and I were invited to participate in an unusual event at the Whitney Museum in New York City for their biennial, and a special CD they planned to issue. The museum put together an exhibit of the artist Joseph Cornell (1903-1972), who collected odd objects and used Surrealism techniques to create assemblages and collages. In his day, Cornell's work was considered to be quite avant garde.

Two persons from California conceived of and organized an experiment for the Whitney. They selected a number of gifted psychics and mediums to remote view some of Cornell's work at the museum and record their impressions for the CD, which would go on display with photographs of the art. Visitors could put on earphones and listen to the mediums' impressions while they looked at the photographs. After its run in New York City, the exhibit was scheduled to tour around the United States and other countries. This was quite a prestigious invitation for us, and we were selected as the top of our field in the New York area.

We had independent sessions for the experiment, in which we were ushered into a room at the Whitney where a box contained Cornell's work. Neither of us was familiar with Cornell, so we had no preconceived ideas of what might be inside the box. We sat at a distance from the box, and were supposed to use our psychic ability to "see" inside.

In comparing our notes later, Karl and I had overlapping impressions. In addition, Karl had been able to remotely view the top of the open box and accurately see and describe the objects inside. Both of us received impressions about Cornell and how he did his work. I was acutely aware of the artist's retiring personality, speech pattern, and his habit of spending much of his time walking on the beach to collect objects. Karl was able to see his studio and described his personal habits. Cornell seemed to effect a "crazy artist" demeanor, perhaps as a way of getting attention. Karl could see him interacting in this persona with clients and members of the art community. Karl also saw Cornell spending time searching for objects for his art, but in a different way: roaming the streets going through garbage cans.

When we were done, we were told by one of the organizers of the experiment that our accuracy was astounding, far more than any of the other mediums.

At another time, we went to see the New Jersey house of a client of mine, whom Karl identifies with the pseudonym Angela Webb in this book. She was a fascinating woman. She was a successful financial trader, and also experienced "time-slips." Her house was haunted and she was quite comfortable with the many personalities who shared her home. While walking through the house by ourselves, Karl and I were struck by something strange in the front room sitting area. I became aware that a woman in a rocking chair was, on some level, still there. Karl actually saw her. When I "see" things at a distance, it is in my mind's eye. Karl sees with his actual eyes.

As Karl and I reach a wider and wider audience, we encourage people to look more closely at the world of the paranormal, and even go so far as to acknowledge that the spirit world is all around us. Our work is often difficult, and sometimes even misunderstood, but we are glad to be pioneers in the field, helping others in their personal lives, and helping many more gain a deeper understanding of the unseen world.

Introduction

I grew up in a time when the general opinion of psychics was that they were turban-wearing scam artists. In New Jersey, where I grew up, the seaside boardwalk during the summer held multiple "psychic" women, seated in small booths, wearing dresses decorated with patterns of stars and moons, reading palms and foretelling the future, all for just a few dollars.

Television shows hosted regular psychic guests like "The Amazing Criswell," the stage name of Jeron Criswell King (born Jeron Criswell Konig). The Amazing Criswell was active from the 1950s to the 1970s, making regular predictions about the future. He was a popular guest on *The Jack Paar Program*, and made several appearances on *The Tonight Show* with Johnny Carson. He was most famous for an uncanny prediction he made on March 10, 1963, on a Jack Paar TV special: "I predict that President Kennedy will not run for re-election in 1964 because of something that will happen to him in November, 1963."

Some of his predictions were outlandish, such as the Great Lakes would become beds of sand because of a massive drought in 1977, and that Las Vegas would have the first Interplanetary Convention on March 10, 1990, with representatives from Neptune, Mars, Venus, and the moon. He also boldly predicted that the end of the world would happen on August 18, 1999.

TV psychics such as Criswell were fun to watch, and many people took *all* the predictions seriously.

Films in that era, the mid-twentieth century, did little to improve the reputation of psychics. Instead, they often portrayed them as shameless scam artists trying to rid gullible people of their money. No wonder that many people were convinced that all psychics were fakes and phonies.

So imagine a boy from Newark, New Jersey coming to grips with the fact that he really can do psychic things, but he cannot tell anyone, because they will think he is either lying or nuts!

That boy was me, Karl Petry, and as a child, I always believed that everybody could do what I could do, see what I could see, and hear what I could hear. I found out, after years of being ridiculed by my family and friends, that this was not the case. It took nearly forty long years for me to believe that people might be ready to hear what I had to say without laughing at me or, worse, mistrusting me.

Slowly, I started to seek out people who had psychic abilities like I did, or people who would not be judgmental and who would believe in me. When my confidence was strong enough, I began to accept invitations to be a presenter at the growing number of ghost hunting and paranormal group conferences. As my popularity grew, I began offering a series of presentations, where I would tell the audiences about my psychic experiences and investigations.

While doing this, I discovered something shocking: people are fascinated with the paranormal, and with very few exceptions, they are supportive of me. Many have sought me out after hearing me speak, to assist them with what they suspected was a paranormal presence in their homes or in other locations.

Many people are searching for explanations for their own experiences with the spirit world. They seem relieved to find that my presentations offer them a forum where they can talk about their experiences, confirm that what they have experienced truly involved the paranormal, and talk to me about their most secret, hidden concerns about what lies beyond this life. Some people have asked for my help in locating cherished lost items and missing people, and in making contact with departed loved ones. I have been very successful in helping many who have asked for my help.

I have never charged money to anyone who has come to me for help. I have declined any payment for my services for a very simple reason: once a person pays a psychic for a reading or for assistance with an intrusive spirit, the customer expects instant results, usually to confirm his or her own theory of what the phenomenon is. In my experience, sometimes I am able to produce results swiftly; more often, however, a real paranormal investigation may take much longer to yield real results. Sometimes there are no results at all.

Sadly, when there is money involved, many psychics, talented or not, feel they must put on a "dog and pony" show for the paying customer. Should the psychic give the verdict of "no ghost" being present, the customer might be convinced he was cheated and that he had picked a "bad" psychic. So, I do not accept payment for my involvement. Oddly, some believe that my refusal of payment means that I am not a "real" psychic, but with most people, this has actually encouraged them to trust me.

One of the pitfalls of doing live presentations is that these events allow me to speak for only short periods of time. I cannot possibly go into great detail about any one subject or story without seeing, out of the corner of my eye, someone standing off stage, pointing to his watch, signaling that I should speak at warp speed because my allotted time is running out. That is why writing this book seemed like the most natural, logical thing for me to do. On these pages, I can go into greater detail about the events and investigations that are special to me, and it also offers me the opportunity to share with you, my readers, what it was like growing up as a clairvoyant and psychic medium.

In this book, I describe my early days of growing up in the Ironbound Section of Newark, New Jersey, my family background, and my struggle to find people I could tell about my psychic abilities without being judged. Fortunately, I was able to find people who gave me guidance and much needed moral support, which in turn enabled me to reach out and help others. I have selected some of my best and most interesting cases.

In my travels, I have met many people who are like me in many ways, but who are as afraid as I once was to share their paranormal abilities and experiences with others. They have, as I did, remained silent, out of fear of ridicule. I am convinced that most people do have varying degrees of psychic ability, but are "forced into hiding" by our skeptical and judgmental society. It is my hope that *Absent Witness* will encourage many of these "closet" psychics to feel confident enough to confide in friends and family about their abilities. Others, I hope, will find a new way of looking at psychics and at the many varieties of psychic ability.

My life could have turned out differently if it were not for my very strong support team. These people are my heroes, and I owe them my thanks and admiration for being open-minded and encouraging. With all my heart, I thank the late Ingo Swann, Dr. Joanne D.S. McMahon, Paula Roberts, Noreen Renier, Karen McLean, Dr. Stephen Braude, Rosemary Ellen Guiley, and, of course, my wife, Dr. Sueli S. Petry. I am especially deeply indebted to Karen McLean, who provided countless hours of support, encouragement, and help with the writing of this book.

—Karl Petry

1

The Soul-Eating House

There are many haunted houses, but there are a rare few that capture and imprison the souls of their owners when they die.

They are "soul-eating" houses, and they have long, troubled histories. I discovered such a house myself, in an emotional and turbulent case wrapped in the tragedy of the 9-11 World Trade Center destruction in New York City. That soul-eating house still stands in New Jersey, and whenever I go by it, I can see the ghost of the woman I knew, who has joined other ghosts held captive in that strange place.

On that sunny morning of September 11, 2001, I joined millions of people around the world to watch in utter horror as terrorists slammed two jumbo jets into the World Trade Center towers. Fire and smoke poured out of the wreckage. On the top floors of the North Tower were the offices of a financial investment company that employed Angela Webb. Part of me prayed that perhaps she had not gone to work that day, but psychically, I knew she had, and she was doomed. Angela burned to death, and her house took her soul.

The story of Angela Webb—a pseudonym I have used to protect the woman's identity—is unique because it is a ghost story that spans over a hundred years. It is also a ghost story that has no end.

Angela Webb was the most haunting case of my career, and it landed on my doorstep just as I was going public with my psychic ability. At the time, it seemed I was drawn into it by chance, but I know now that nothing ever happens by chance.

My involvement began over a few glasses of champagne I had at a gathering in 2001 at the Manhattan apartment of a parapsychologist I knew, Victoria Wright. Victoria was known to all as "Vicki." Her apartment was in the theater district, and, from her balcony, you got a bird's eye view of the busy streets that encompass the 42nd Street area.

Vicki became intrigued by the paranormal when she took a course in parapsychology while studying at the City University of New York (CUNY). She later received her Ph.D. in basic and applied neurocognition. Over the years, Vicki was involved with paranormal investigations and, from time to time, made appearances on television.

Vicki invited people who were involved with parapsychology to gather at her apartment one Saturday night in an informal salon to discuss their latest projects in the field. I drove in from New Jersey with parapsychologist Dr. Joanne D.S. McMahon of the Parapsychology Foundation. Joanne was a friend of Vicki's, and I came along as her guest. A get-together of this type was a first for me.

I recalled seeing Vicki briefly at the Parapsychology Foundation months earlier. At the time, I didn't know who she was—until I heard someone call out her name. "Vicki" is not a common name, so it stuck in my head. Vicki was a few years older than me, an attractive woman with dark hair and a fondness for champagne. It was no surprise, then, to find that everyone who walked into her apartment that night brought a bottle or two.

After introductions, we gathered in the parlor where the furniture was arranged in a circle. Vicki wanted everyone attending her party to have his say in the circle. Rather than letting people talk over each other, Vicki had created a method to keep order during the discussion. It involved a small, primitive-looking statue. The statue would be handed from one person to the next. Once it was placed in your hand, it was your turn to talk. When you were finished, you passed it to the person on your right, and so on. It was her version of the "talking stick," a similar prop used in many therapy and self-help circles.

Even before we got started, most everyone had a glass of bubbly in his or her hand, and a few had their cheese and crackers balanced on their knees. As I was taking my seat, I noticed Paula, a woman I had been briefly introduced to as I arrived. She was not sitting in the circle, but at the kitchen table. Paula was about five feet nine inches tall with blonde hair, blue eyes and a sophisticated English accent. She was tastefully dressed in a pants suit.

Soon, the statue was making its rounds, and the subjects discussed ranged from what books the speaker was reading, to personal views of recent lectures he or she had attended, to lively debate about conflicting views of the current research in the field.

After the third guest spoke, the statue came into my hand. Dr. McMahon had already warned me of what to expect at this party, and I thought it was a good opportunity to openly confer with these knowledgeable people about psychic phenomena.

I stared at the primitive idol in my lap as I tried to figure out where to begin. Without diverting my eyes from the statue, I dove right into my day-to-day difficulties living as a psychic. I spoke about the fear of social ridicule and all the sleepless nights caused by strange images whirling through my head. I ended with a few of the positive accomplishments made possible by my ability. When I finished, a voice from the crowd said, "Now pass the statue to your right." No one said a word to me about what I had just confessed, no comments or questions, just the sound of more champagne being poured before the talks continued. I was shocked to see that no one asked any questions or made a comment from my confession.

About an hour later we took a break. I walked across the floor, champagne glass in hand, to the balcony that overlooked 43rd street. I was taking in the view when Paula walked up to me and said, "Pearls before swine." She repeated a bid louder, "Pearls before swine!"

At first I didn't get it. With a half-smile she said, "They didn't hear a word you were saying." She then reintroduced herself to me.

Paula Roberts was a famous psychic often written about in the New York newspapers. She was the friend of the *New York Post* columnist Cindy Adams, and her New Year's predictions were always printed in the newspaper. Her prediction accuracy was very high. Paula was the only person in the room who understood my plight. For the rest of the night, we discussed our mutual psychic abilities and activities. I was impressed that Paula could see into the future as well as the past, and she was equally impressed that I could actually see entities and not just feel them.

Paula Roberts

Soon I would discover that the day I met Paula Roberts would turn out to be a monumental day in my life. In the weeks and months that followed, I found Paula Roberts and Joanne McMahon always there for me, giving me emotional support. Things began to look much better. I was a person who had, for years, shied away from any type of psychic fame, and now I started a life of psychic openness.

When Paula and I met, I was working on my own locally aired cable television show, *Strange Dimensions*, which featured paranormal topics and personalities, including authors and musicians. Paula seemed like an ideal guest, so I added her to the roster of my regulars who did segments on the show. She was a big hit with the audience. *Strange Dimensions* gave us an opportunity to become closer friends.

The Angela Webb case started early on a Thursday afternoon, in May 2001. I was working on an old radio I had just found. In this age of computers, transistors, iPods and cell phones, I still spent a good amount of time repairing and collecting old tube radios. I had just slashed my index finger when it slipped off my pliers and struck a sharp metal corner of the radio chassis. When I saw my blood oozing onto the wiring of the radio, I ran to the kitchen holding my finger and grabbed a paper towel off the dispenser. I slowed the flow of blood long enough to secure an adhesive bandage onto my finger. I took another paper towel and was dabbing the blood off the tubes and wires, when the phone rang.

Annoyed at the interruption, I must have sounded like a madman when I answered the phone with a loud and angry, "Hello!"

There was no reply for a moment, then I heard a woman with an English accent say, "Karl?"

It was Paula. I apologized for my rude manner of answering the telephone, and explained my predicament.

Paula lightly brushed it off and told me about her client, "Angela." As I mentioned, this is a pseudonym, and as this story unfolds, you will understand why I choose not to use her real name.

Paula told me that, during a reading she was doing for Angela, she told her, "You are surrounded by many people in your home."

Angela answered, "But I live alone."

Paula, sticking to her original comment, argued, "But I see you living with many people."

Angela then answered, "Well, if you count the ghosts in the house, I do."

Paula asked in a questioning voice, "Ghosts?"

Angela smiled, "Ghosts. Wall to wall ghosts! Would you like to see them?"

"Yes!" said Paula.

Paula asked me if I would be interested in researching this house with her.

Without hesitation I answered, "Yes!" This was the start of a strange and compelling investigation that I would later refer to as "The Ghosts of Angela Webb."

As an additional incentive, I still had the cable show and this investigation would give me video footage of our investigation. No matter if there was a ghost or not, I would have a least three shows' worth of footage.

On a serious note, Angela believed she had ghosts in her house, and she felt extremely fortunate that two of us would be there to investigate. Rarely on any ghost investigation are there two psychics working together, side by side.

Was Angela truthful? Was her house really packed "wall-to-wall" with spirits, as she claimed? Could it be something else?

Most haunted houses feature residues rather than active ghosts. Residual hauntings are imprints of activities that once took place over and over in a location. When the people pass on, their ghost-like imprints remain, like looped recordings.

For example, once when I was attending a party, I saw an imprint of a man wearing a hat and overcoat walk through the front door to the closet, where he removed his hat and placed it on the left hand side of the shelf in the closet. He then took his coat off, placed it on a hanger, and hung it up. Then the image disappeared. About a minute later, the whole sequence started over again.

I told the host of the party what I saw. She, in turn, told the landlord, who had previously lived in the house. The landlord confirmed that the image was that of her father, and that he had always entered the house after work, removed his hat and coat, and put them in the closet just as I described.

That is a classic imprint or residual haunting. An imprint goes on about its business, repeating a task without notice of the living. Real ghosts, on the other hand, react to the living and what is happening in a location. Some ghosts do not like the living invading their space, and will act up, which creates a different kind of haunting.

I was curious to find out what Angela had going on in her house filled with many ghosts.

Paula arranged a date and time for our visit with Angela. On a Saturday morning, Paula took a bus to New Jersey, and I picked her up in my freshly washed and vacuumed 1983 gold and black Chevy Blazer. It was packed with a video camera, still camera, a light package, and various microphones. In a few minutes, we were on Route 78 heading west toward Pennsylvania.

The trip took just over an hour. Angela told us her house was located about a quarter-mile from the Delaware River, which borders Pennsylvania. Her directions took us through small towns near the Pennsylvania border and up a huge mountain. I had never traveled in this part of the state, and many of the roads did not have road signs. Concentrating on the complex directions kept me focused on the road, and kept our conversation focused on what turn to make next. The radio served as background music for most of the trip until the signal got weak as we reached the tall mountains near the Pennsylvania border. Now, with the radio signal fading out and with my tape player broken, I turned the radio off.

Finally, we were on the road nearing Angela's house, a two-lane, blacktop country road with numbered metal mailboxes lining the shoulder. We were told to look for a barn with an unfinished American flag painted on the side. Her house would be next to it. We came to a spot on the road where the trees bent inward, reaching from both sides, which made a sort of tree tunnel with a weird, almost otherworldly feel to it. Through that and to the right was the American flag barn. I slowed to a crawl past the barn, and there, true to Angela's description, stood her house.

I turned into the driveway and was relieved that we hadn't gotten lost. Paula and I got out of the truck. I glanced over and saw her looking at the massive grounds of the house. To the right stood the huge barn, and in between that and the house was a flower garden. I opened the tailgate and began removing my camera equipment. This old, two-story farmhouse looked to be in excellent condition. The grounds were manicured, and I could see that the house had a fresh coat of paint on it.

Oddly, it had not one but two wooden front doors, side by side. I was about twenty feet from the house when, from the corner of my eye, I saw a young boy standing next to the porch, staring at me. Before I could focus on him, his image disappeared.

In lock step, Paula and I put our right feet on the porch at the same time. When the sole of my shoe touched the porch, my head began to spin. I desperately held on to the tripod and camera case, trying not to fall. I looked at Paula—she was having a similar reaction. She swung around and grabbed one of the columns holding up the porch, to prevent her from falling.

We were both dazed and, as we were mentally recovering, Paula said, "It seems we're at the right house."

No doubt in my mind, we certainly were. In all my years of doing this work, nothing like this had ever happened to me before. Paula and I stood motionless, looking at the two front doors in front of us. Looking back, it sounds strange even to me, but for a moment we had to decide: "Which door do we knock on?"

Paula took the initiative and knocked on the right side door. Angela answered. She was about five-foot-four with long and thick dark hair worn straight down. She had dark eyes that peeked through her hair.

I never quite heard how she greeted us, because the moment the door was opened, I could see, over her right shoulder, a woman dressed in a white gown. She was standing in the middle of the living room, staring at us.

The woman in white was a ghost. The image of this woman was as clear to me as Angela and Paula. I kept my vision secret, and did not say a word as we entered the living room. This ghost did not disappear, but walked around us. I knew immediately that this was a rare "intelligent haunting," because this spirit was interacting with us.

When Angela walked away from us for a few seconds, Paula turned to me and said, "I feel a presence around us—it's a woman."

Once again, Paula was right on target. I shared with her what I was experiencing, but cut my conversation short when Angela walked back into the room. In a flash, the spirit was gone.

Angela gave us a tour. Besides the three of us, a mother cat with her newborn kittens were the only other living creatures in the house. Angela told us of her experiences with various ghosts since moving in a few years earlier. She knew that we would be taking pictures and videotaping, and told us to feel free to do whatever we wanted. She said she had an appointment and had to run, but we could stay. If we left before she returned, we should just lock the door as we left.

Paula and I knew the ghosts in the house were watching us. I repeat: "ghosts," plural. There were more than one, and we knew it. We proceeded to set up for the taping. As I was mounting my camera onto the tripod, I could feel eyes watching me, seemingly from all corners of the room. When it came to being haunted, we knew that this house was the real thing. Angela's earlier comments about her house having ghosts, on the day Paula first read her, had been no exaggeration.

I positioned the camera and tested the microphone as Paula stood in front of the camera. Paula was no stranger to the television camera; she knew what to do without my telling her. By being good with a microphone and camera, she saved me a great deal of time when I edited my show. Once I gave her the sign that the camera was rolling, she began by telling the viewers all about this beautiful house in Western New Jersey, and that we were experiencing ghostly happenings. Then suddenly, just after Paula's introduction, a loud noise sounded in the second floor. It was as if a huge person had jumped from a ladder or dresser onto the floor, directly above us. We were startled by this loud crash. Paula, the trouper she was, remarked casually, "I know that sound you just heard was a cat living upstairs with its new litter of kittens." Paula knew it wasn't the cat or the kittens, but wanted to make a comment for the audience as an explanation to the sound they just heard.

From behind the camera I looked up at her and mouthed the word, "Cats?" for if it was a cat that made that noise, it would have had to have been a lion weighing over two hundred pounds! A few seconds later, the frail mother cat was rubbing against Paula's leg, proving it hadn't been the cat at all that we had heard on the second floor. No. Whatever was on the second floor was warning us.

Paula and I began our inspection of each room located on the first floor. Paula gave her impressions of the furnishings and appearances of the inhabitants in the early days of this farm house, while I kept the camera in focus and the audio levels within their proper ranges. She was doing an excellent job hosting this haunted tour. Her English accent gave her ghostly observations more credibility. If I'm in front of the camera, there is always a danger of my breaking into my "Newark-ese" accent, which would make our entire venture look like one of the old "Bowery Boys" films from the 1940s!

When we took a break from shooting, I ventured to the second floor. I began hearing voices and seeing images. There was a window that had a view of the barn, and I could see the woman in white, sitting on a small chair, looking out toward the barn. The window glass was wavy, common to glass after about a hundred years of settling in a window frame. I stood a few feet behind her and peered over her shoulder to see what she was looking at. There was a large man wearing a straw hat, walking from the house to the barn. The ghost woman began having a mental dialogue with me.

In a soft, sad voice, she said, "This man will have his way with me tonight. He is not my uncle as he says, but just my father's helper who lives with us. My father knows and does nothing to help me."

I could feel her fright and sorrow. I felt totally helpless. How could I help a person who experienced this over a hundred years ago? Was I caught in some kind of vortex that repeats time from the past, over and over? Whatever this was, this young woman had been experiencing this horror repeatedly, since it first started over a century ago. I was an absent witness to this woman being violated. With great sadness, I left her at the window and proceeded downstairs. As I approached the spiral staircase to return to the first floor, I turned and saw the woman still staring at the barn, paying no attention to me. I was the intruder from the future who could not save her from the unfortunate fate of her past.

With each step I took down those stairs, a flood of images raced through my mind. This woman and maybe the other entities were transmitting information to me at a remarkable speed. Can you imagine "living" as a ghost, unable to communicate with anyone for almost two centuries, and then having someone you can communicate with suddenly walk into your life? I was that somebody, and I would carry those horrid, rapid-fire images for the rest of my life.

I did not tell Paula what had happened upstairs. That could wait for our ride home. So, after our break, we continued shooting the video. As we faced the kitchen from the dining room, we heard the kitchen door open, and the sound of a person walking into the room. Paula smiled at the camera and said, "Our host has just arrived and I'm sure you would like to meet her."

With the camera still rolling, we waited, but Angela Webb did not walk into the room. She could not, because she was not there. She was still away and out of the house. What opened the door and walked into the room is unknown, but we recorded the event, which proved, at least to us, that it really did happen.

I picked up the camera and tripod and moved toward the barn, which was enormous. It was two stories tall and in relatively good shape. Paula walked into the barn first with me following about twenty feet behind. She said she had an eerie feeling about the place. Just as I walked in, I could see a man hanging from the upper beam. Before I could say a single word, Paula said, "I sense death here, a man hanging." I confirmed what she saw and described the man in detail. I thought that the man who was hanging in the barn was the same man who had worked as a helper many years ago, and the man who violated the woman of the house.

Angela's house was built a few centuries ago when the entire area was isolated. Any hired help must have lived in the house—and what type of help were they getting? We take precautions about who we hire to work on and in our homes now, but how about then? I am sure they were happy to get anyone with a strong back to work the farm, but these workers could have had some serious mental health problems. To take it one step further, if you were the woman living in this house back then, what would you do to save yourself from a predator like this man? Would you be able to walk for miles in the dark to get to another house? And if you managed to get to that house, would the neighbors believe your story of cruelty by a farmhand or a father? Let's face it: probably not. They would send you to the minister to see if he could pray for you so that your sanity would return. Back then, there was a bleak outcome for any woman going through this.

Angela returned to the house shortly after we finished the taping. She told us of her haunting experiences in the house. We kept the ghostly events we had experienced to ourselves.

Angela said the activity began the day she bought the house in 1998. The real estate agent met her at the house after she had signed the paperwork and officially owned it. The previous owner and his daughter stopped by to remove a few items they had left behind.

The little girl walked up to Angela and asked, "Are you the lady that bought my daddy's house?"

Angela answered, "Yes I am."

The little girl said, "Do you want to meet my friends?"

With a huge smile Angela answered, "Yes I would."

The girl took Angela up the spiral stairway to the second floor, to the first bedroom on the right.

"This was my room," the child told Angela.

The room was painted pink and a shelf circled the entire room about eighteen inches from the ceiling. Her stuffed dolls and animals were still perched on the shelf all the way around.

"So these are your friends," Angela said.

"No, these are my toys," the girl answered. "This is my friend, and his name is Jason." She pointed to an empty rocking chair in the room. Angela thought the girl had an imaginary friend and decided to play along with it.

She bent down to the chair and said, "Hello! My name is Angela and I'll be living here now."

The little girl looked very upset at Angela, as if she was making fun of her.

They both went downstairs where the father was waiting. He and his daughter quickly said their goodbyes and left, leaving many pieces of furniture and other items, including all the dolls and stuffed animals in the girl's room. Angela stayed at the house that night and slept in the little girl's room, because it was the only room that had a bed in it; her furniture would not be delivered for a few days.

In the early hours of the next day, just as the sun was rising, Angela was awakened by a squeaky sound in the room. She opened her eyes to see a boy rocking in the rocking chair, staring at her. You would think that if a woman were awakened by a ghost, she would leap out of bed and dash out the door, screaming at the top of her lungs. But this was not Angela's way. She stared back at Jason until he faded out, then got out of bed to start her day.

As Paula and I stood in front of the property, Angela continued to tell us of the strange things that had happened to her in and around the house. On one particular day, Angela had taken on the task of pruning her enormous garden. She worked from morning to sundown. She had only one bush left, but it was too dark to continue, so this last bush would have to wait until the next morning to be pruned.

Early the next morning, with her pruning tools in hand, Angela approached the bush. To her shock, it was totally pruned. Who—or what—had finished the job?

She also told us the story about the American flag that was painted on the side of her barn. After she bought the property, Angela wanted an artist to paint a huge flag on the barn. Through word of mouth, she found someone named Robert, who took on the job. He was a good-looking man in his thirties, and had a great reputation for his skill as an artist and his strong commitment to always complete the jobs he took on.

During the weekdays, Angela worked in New York City, where she also had an apartment. She came out to this, her country home, on weekends, holidays, and vacations. This worked out well for Robert, because he liked working without interruptions. For days he chalked out his pattern for the flag, climbing up and down his huge aluminum ladder, making sure he did not miss a single detail.

A few days later, when Angela came out to the house, Robert told her about the boy who watched him work from the side of the house.

"He doesn't say anything, he just watches," Robert said.

Angela paid it no mind, thinking that the boy was the neighbor's son who lived across the road.

After a week of chalking his project, Robert began mixing the paint for the job. At first things went well. He figured the boy had lost interest in the project because he no longer showed up. Then, out of nowhere, the boy made his appearance. This time the boy approached the ladder. Robert politely told the boy not to stand next to the ladder in case he dropped something, and, if he stood too close, the paint might splatter him. The boy just focused his eyes on Robert without saying a word. Then, in what seemed like a split second, the boy disappeared. Robert was unnerved, and preferred not to think about what happened. He kept working.

A few days later, the flag was taking shape and the weather seemed to be cooperating with the project. If all went well, with no rain to delay his work, the job would be finished by the end of the week.

The next day, Robert raised his ladder against the barn and climbed to the top with his paint can and brushes. He was startled to see the boy suddenly present. This time, the boy started shaking the ladder, so violently that Robert feared he would fall.

"Get away from here! Are you trying to kill me?" Robert yelled.

The boy would not stop shaking the ladder. Robert started climbing down. The boy ran away, dashing around the corner of the house. Robert ran to catch him, but the boy had disappeared.

When his nerves were back to normal, Robert climbed back up the ladder and continued his painting. He was three quarters completed when the boy showed up again. Robert did not notice him until the ladder began to shake. In a heightened state of anger, he threw the paintbrush at the boy and descended the ladder as fast as he could.

The boy did not run, but slowly walked away towards the corner of the house, as he had previously. When Robert turned the corner, the boy just stood there, with his arms at his sides facing him, almost as if he were challenging Robert. Before one word came out of Robert's mouth, the boy just faded away.

Judging by his description of the boy, Angela knew it was the ghost of Jason, the little girl's friend who liked to rock in the rocking chair in her room.

Robert packed his unused paint, took his equipment and left, vowing never to return. Angela paid him for the work he had completed, and that was the reason for the unfinished American flag on the side of the barn.

Angela offered us some tea, so we went back into the house. We gathered in the kitchen, where she continued to tell us of her ghostly encounters. The kitchen was the only room that had been modernized, and was equipped with the latest appliances. There was an island in the middle of the kitchen, which also served as a working counter for food preparation or as an eating area. The latter seemed to be the most popular use for it, because there were tall, white stools in the front of the island where we sat. Angela stood facing us from the opposite side of the island. Behind me was a stone bookcase built into the wall. Each shelf was lined with cookbooks and decorative, small knick-knacks.

Tea was served; I left my teabag soaking longer in the cup than Paula did, because I like my tea strong. With all that had gone on during this trip, I was looking forward to a nice, strong cup of tea.

During our conversation with Angela, I kept seeing disturbing images of a sexual nature that involved our host. I wanted to ask the question but I needed to phrase my question in such a way that it did not come across as crude or brash. So I looked up from my teacup and asked her, "Have you ever been intimate with an entity here?"

Paula turned her head and looked at me as if I had lost my mind. To our surprise, Angela answered quickly, and without missing a beat went right to the point. "Yes I have."

The disturbing image I was seeing was verified. There was nothing meek about Angela—she was a tough-talking gal who came right to the point. I could see a deep unease in Paula the same uneasiness I was feeling. It seemed we both felt an unsettling presence around us but did not want to mention it to Angela.

Angela did not offer details about her sexual experiences with the ghosts, but I had impressions that she had had multiple encounters.

When my tea had had sufficient time to darken, I removed the teabag and placed it on the saucer. I calmly glanced up at Paula, and she returned my glance, acknowledging the same feelings we both were experiencing.

Suddenly, the books in the bookcase behind us started to slam from the left side of the bookcase to the right, and continued from shelf to shelf, making an ungodly noise! Paula and I jumped to our feet and backed away from the bookcase. We turned to Angela, who had little to no reaction to this terrifying event.

Paula said, "Doesn't this bother you?"

Angela answered, "No. This happens all the time."

Paula then said, "How can you live in a house where this happens all the time?"

To our surprise, Angela answered with an angry tone to her voice, "I tell them, 'This is my house! I paid for it! I want you to stop this right now!'"

Obviously, Paula's question had hit a nerve with Angela, but her ranting continued. "I tell them, 'If you don't stop this, I'll get a dog and you'll have to deal with that! I'll bring in children, too!'"

As strange as it seemed, Angela obviously liked her ghosts and did not fear them. She and her ghosts appeared to co-exist in this house without a problem—or at least a significant one as far as Angela was concerned.

Angela told us that sometimes all the books came out of the bookcase and flew around the room, and had even "flown" as far as the next room. After hearing this, there was no doubt in our minds that there were multiple hauntings in this house. This was not the one female ghost—the "woman in white"—having a temper tantrum. This was the action of a strong male presence, and it was not the child-ghost Jason, either. Paula and I could feel a new entity, a strong personality with an edge of meanness, taunting us by showing off of its strength with the slamming of the books. This ghost stayed invisible even to me. I sensed that our having a conversation about the haunting with Angela was making him upset.

Paula's comment to Angela during her reading, that "she was surrounded by many people," rang true again. Angela was surrounded by ghosts, many ghosts, and we were not the only ones other than Angela who had experienced them. Angela told us of one of her early encounters with the ghosts and the people who were the unwilling witnesses—friends who were party guests.

What good is a beautiful home if you can't have your friends over for a party every now and then? Angela told her co-workers about her newly-purchased country home and the ghosts that inhabited it. They laughed and made cutting remarks about her "haunted house," but accepted Angela's invitation for a party she was having over a particular weekend.

Things unraveled late in the evening of the first night. One of the guests asked Angela if he could spend the night there because he was leaving for Washington, D.C., early the next morning and wanted to have enough sleep before he started his trip. A few of the others also decided to stay, since the party lasted well into the early hours of the morning.

About four o'clock in the morning, a scream rang out from one of the guest rooms: "Angela! Angela!"

Angela rushed to the room where her friend was sleeping. She threw open his door and saw him huddled at the end of the bed, clutching the blanket.

"There was a guy standing next to the bed staring at me, it looked like he was going to kill me," her friend quavered. "Then he disappeared. It was horrible!"

With his eyes wide open he went on, "When the sun comes up, I'll be out of here! What happens here when the lights go out is terrifying!"

Before Angela could say a word, there was another scream from another guest. She ran down the second floor hall, only to see one of the women on all fours, crawling down the staircase head first in a continuous scream. Angela pulled her up from the stairs and guided her to a chair.

The woman kept saying, "Get me out of here! Get me out of here! Please, please, just get me out of here!"

By now everyone in the house was awake and Angela was trying hard to calm everyone down. Nothing could be done with the woman, who was in shock. An ambulance was called and the woman was taken to a nearby hospital and treated. Within a few hours, everyone who had stayed overnight was gone. After that, no co-worker would come back to Angela's house, and the teasing in the office about her "haunted house" ended.

Angela did not reveal to us any details of what exactly had frightened her friends so badly.

After all that happened, Angela wanted to do some investigation herself about this mysterious property she had bought. The township where her house was located did not have a historical society or museum. A few miles down the road from her were a small library, a firehouse, and an old church, which stood across the road from the Delaware River. One day Angela decided to stop by the church and talk to the pastor or caretakers to see if they knew something about her house and the people who had lived there. She met a woman there who considered herself a historian for the area.

"When I told her who I was and the house I lived in, she had plenty of information for me," Angela said. "She told me about a boy many years ago who was run over by a car and killed. Then she went on about a woman who was a nymphomaniac who had disappeared in the 1940s. Her husband claimed that she had left him and returned to her family in the Midwest. No one had ever investigated his claim, but there were rumors that he killed her and buried her on this property."

The woman also told Angela of the many families that lived in her house over the years. Angela asked this woman how she knew so much information about her house. The woman answered that everyone who had ever bought the house sooner or later wanted the same information, and the search always ended up at this church.

As Angela went on, detailing the history she had discovered about previous occupants of the house—who now seemed to be ghostly residents—a disturbing picture emerged. Over and over again, others had warned her not to stay in the house because tragic ends came to those who owned it, yet she shrugged off the warnings. She had gotten sucked into a phantom twilight zone, from which she either could not, or would not, free herself. Even her motives for calling us to the scene were unclear. Angela did not need us to tell her the house was haunted—she was deeply engaged in a relationship with her ghosts. She had not asked us to clear the ghosts. What did she want from us? Many people who contact paranormal investigators really do not want their ghosts to go away—they want attention and hope to be on television. This was not the case with Angela. She relished her privacy. Now she was letting us into her private world, and was even agreeable to a British television program featuring her house.

After Paula and I left Angela's house that day, we rode quietly in the truck for a number of miles. What we had experienced was unsettling. We had the distinct impression that the house was a ghost prison of sorts, holding the souls of those who had been associated with it at the time of their deaths. If you died while you owned the house or had a strong association with it—regardless of where and how you died—the house claimed you. It seemed to both of us that the house, or its ghosts, gave us a warning not to return. Yet, we both agreed that if Angela extended to us another invitation, we would come back. A house with blatant physical paranormal phenomena happening before our eyes was something this pair of psychics would not want to miss.

Paula called Angela the following day. As we expected, she said that we could stop by anytime she was there.

Before we proceeded, Paula took some time off to visit her family in England. On her return flight to the States, she met a woman named Elaine who was a producer for Granada Television in England. Paula told her about this extraordinary haunted house in New Jersey. Elaine was immediately interested in doing a show about it. Before Elaine could sell this haunted house show to her people at Granada, however, she had to make sure that both Paula and I were "real" psychics.

Paula phoned me and related her meeting with Elaine, and asked if I would mind if she videotaped us using our psychic abilities. I agreed without hesitation.

The next day, we were asked to meet at an apartment house in Manhattan on the Upper East Side. We did not know that this was Elaine's apartment, which she shared with another woman named Dawn. I met Paula at her apartment and then we walked to the destination apartment house, which was not far. The doorman was expecting us and let us into the lobby, and told us the floor and apartment number where we were to meet Elaine. When we reached the apartment, Elaine and Dawn greeted us. With them were two video camera operators. Elaine said that we would be split up, and a camera would follow each one of us around the apartment as we gave our psychic impressions. We were never to be in the same room together so that we could not hear what the other was saying.

We agreed and started our individual tours. Dawn followed me along with a camera operator. Paula went with Elaine and the other camera operator.

My first stop was into an empty room. I could see, in my mind, that at one time there had been a desk in the center of the room, and I saw a man sitting behind it. I described the man in detail. I went on to say that the entire room was filled with paper and that there was a huge amount of child pornography in it. I added that this man was not trustworthy and was a thief.

Dawn, noticeably shaken by my comments, turned toward the door and left the room without saying a word. We later switched rooms, and I gave my observation of the room Paula had been in a few minutes earlier. I felt this room was filled with sickness, one that could not be cured. There was a heavy sadness within its walls.

When we finished touring the entire apartment, we all met in the living room. Elaine, Dawn, and the camera operators were amazed at our accuracy. Dawn said that her husband had an office in the apartment and had his desk positioned as I had described. The room was full of files and boxes, almost waist high. Dawn had never interfered with his business until one day, while he was away, she decided to check into what he was doing. She found stacks and stacks of child pornography. She also found out that he had stolen hundreds of thousands of dollars of her money. When he returned, she threw him out of her apartment and they divorced. My clairvoyance had been right on. Paula had fared just as well, giving Dawn an insight into the man's personality. Similar to my perceptions, Paula's were dead-on accurate. We both felt the second room of sickness was there prior to Dawn's rental and would be impossible for us to substantiate our impression.

The female camera operator, after witnessing this experiment, told us about her brother, who had been convicted of killing a man and was in prison. She believed her brother to be innocent, and asked us if we could tell her who was the real killer. I looked at Paula, she looked at me, and we both said together, "Your brother did kill that man."

The woman's only reply was, "Oh."

Now that we had convinced Elaine of our abilities, the next step would be going over the details of the filming with the Granada film crew at the Angela Webb house.

This all took place late August of 2001. Our one and so far only visit to Angela's house had been in May. We had had plenty of time to plan things out. I wanted to gather experts in the field to be present at the shoot, starting with my parapsychologist friend, Joanne D.S. McMahon; paranormal researcher and good friend George Hansen; and Professor Stephen Braude of the University of Maryland, who was deep into the parapsychology field. I wanted every base of this event covered. Phone calls were made to arrange our schedules for a pre-production meeting with Elaine, Angela, Joanne, Paula, and myself.

On Friday August 17, we all met at Paula's apartment in New York City. We decided that I would lead the procession of Granada's trucks, loaded with gear, to Angela's house. The date and time of the shoot and all the incidentals involved were arranged for Saturday, September 29. At the end of the meeting, Elaine asked how she could get in touch with Angela at work in case she had any additional questions.

Angela said, "Here is my business card; you can call me there during the day." I also reached out and took one of her cards, and saw that she worked at One World Trade Center on one of the top floors.

On September 8, Angela called Paula and said that she saw balls of lights circling around her bedroom and disappearing into the walls and closet, and that she was worried and concerned about this. Paula calmed her down and told her not to worry about it. Paula then phoned me and told me the balls of light were a bad sign, an omen of death. Although it was a concern, we left it alone and took no further action.

The morning of September 11 was a shock to the world as we learned that Middle Eastern terrorists hijacked jet airliners and turned them into weapons to crash into both of the World Trade Center towers in New York. Paula called me the minute the first plane hit. We both hoped that Angela had not gone to work that day, or that maybe she was on vacation or out of town on business. Sadly, in our hearts we both knew she was gone. We watched in horror as flames and black smoke poured out of the towers... as desperate victims leaped to their deaths from the upper floors... and then as both towers crumpled, disintegrated, and fell. There was no hope, especially for those on the top floors.

Night after night, I tried to sleep, but horrible visions of Angela's final moments kept me awake. I could mentally see into an office where the suspended ceiling tiles were all on the floor. The wires that held up the drop ceiling frames remained dangling and swaying back and forth. I could smell jet fuel and felt the heat of the fire spreading through the floor. I could see a hand reaching from beneath a desk, grabbing a computer keyboard that was melting from the heat, and I could smell burning hair. I did not want to believe what I was seeing, but there was no use kidding myself. It was Angela. I was watching her die, over and over, day after day. Believe no one who says that being a psychic or medium is a wonderful gift, for it means witnessing something like this.

Angela's body was never recovered. There was a memorial service held for her in her hometown of Harrisburg, Pennsylvania. Paula and I attended this memorial service. It was held at a Catholic church, which was completely filled with mourners. The priest and a few of her friends spoke about the fine person Angela had been and of the tragedy that had caused her death.

Later, we attended a repast at a restaurant a few miles away where Angela's friends and family gathered. No one at our table knew who we were. Paula politely asked if anyone had ever visited Angela's home in New Jersey. The entire table stopped talking, and then everyone turned to her without saying a word. Their reaction was very strange.

When it was time for us to leave, we approached Angela's father and mother to offer our condolences. Her parents looked like hippies, judging by the way they had their hair cut and the clothing they wore.

The mother said, "We know who you are. Angela told us about the two psychics she had at her house and the TV people that were coming to shoot a show there."

Paula asked, "Did you ever visit her home?"

The father said, "Once." Then he looked at his wife and continued, "We were afraid of all the ghosts and wouldn't go back there." As we turned to walk away, the father added, "Looks like the house has one more ghost."

When Paula and I left the restaurant, we met Claire, a close friend of Angela's. Claire told us that Angela's parents were asked by the forensics team handling the identification of the bodies to bring samples of Angela's hair, which could be found on her hairbrush. The hair's DNA could then be matched with the bodies they were finding. Claire said that Angela's parents were so afraid of going into the house that they asked Claire to get the brush. Evidently their fear of the ghosts was genuine.

Paula and I agree that Angela's spirit was back at the house. With all the information we had, including what we observed, it seems the house holds the spirits of those who die while owning it, regardless of where they die. It is a soul-eating house.

Years have passed, and I have spoken to many groups about this haunting, and even made a short film based on it. I have come to the realization that there is no way I can properly describe the feelings I experienced with this house and towards the ghosts that live in it, as well as my feelings about Angela and the images that have forever imprinted themselves into my brain of both her life and tragic death.

In the years that followed, I have driven past the home of Angela a number of times. I said "home," not "former home," because she is still there. On one particular afternoon when I happened to be driving past the house, I pulled over to look at the house maybe for the last time. As my eyes looked up to the second floor window, I saw the image of Angela looking back down on me. If she could read my mind she would have heard me say a number of times, "I'm sorry. I'm so very, very sorry." The image of her in the window was branded into my brain, and I still cannot remember my drive back home that day.

The house has changed hands a number of times since the tragedy of 9-11, and I am sure many more will sign their names on the deed to that property before I am gone. Families do not stay long in this most unusual home.

As I mentioned previously, I did not use Angela's real name. After all these years, the 9-11 tragedy is still very fresh to many, and I do not want to encourage people driving past her house or bothering the neighbors or owners with questions. I never made an attempt to contact any of the new owners of the house.

We always must remember that our investigation of the Angela Webb house is not just a ghost story and should not be taken as such. Angela was a real woman who, by no fault of her own, became mixed in a world of the living and dead. Angela spoke to us frankly about her haunting problem, and she gave Paula and me the utmost respect for who we are. For that, I will always be grateful.

At the memorial service, one of her best friends distributed a CD of Angela's favorite songs, with a card that sums up her life. It read:

> Dear Friends of Angela:
>
> For twenty-nine years I was blessed with a friendship that was fiercely loyal, always comforting and forever entertaining. Angela Webb was an extraordinary woman who touched everyone's life. Her spirit and generosity must be sustained. The songs on this memorial CD were selected for their meaning and the memories they evoke. Music soothed her soul. Let it stimulate your spirit to carry on her work. Angela embraced her life and love and laughter. I will miss her more than words can adequately express.

She was my oldest and dearest friend. Like you, I loved her without limits.
May God continue to bless you and your families!

The Songs:

1. Why	Annie Lennox
2. American Woman	Lenny Kravitz
3. Respect	Aretha Franklin
4. Heart of Gold	Neil Young
5. Strong Enough	Sheryl Crow
6. Satisfaction	Rolling Stones
7. You Are So Beautiful	Joe Cocker
8. Landslide	Fleetwood Mac
9. Let Your Soul Be Your Pilot	Sting
10. I will Remember You	Sarah McLaughlin
11. Honeybee	Tom Petty
12. Big Mistake	Natalie Imbroglia
13. Higher	Creed

Angela Webb-An American Beauty
August __, 19__ - September 11, 2001

Hopefully Angela has found some peace in that community of ghosts. Will she ever move on? At present, it is impossible to say. Her story belongs to strange dimensions, just like the name of my long-ago show.

The Angela Webb case had a tremendous impact on me just as my career as a professional psychic was getting underway. There were other, even stranger cases that followed.

2

The Lost Love of Daisy

The Daisy story is an unusual haunting case, a paranormal investigator's dream, because it has a beginning, middle, and an end. Having all of these three elements in an investigation is exceptionally rare. In the world of the paranormal, the Daisy case is a *classic*.

The case has a human side, too, something paranormal investigators often lose sight of in their rush to collect evidence. Daisy lived her entire life with a wounded heart. The man she loved never came for her, and in death she still pined for him.

My thoughts go back to the morning of December 31, 2012. I'd had many things racing through my mind the night before, and I could not get to sleep until three in the morning. I woke up at about 8 AM with an awful headache. Looking out the window, I saw that two inches of snow had fallen during the night. There was no time to waste. I had to get the sidewalk shoveled before 11:30 AM because that's when my friends, Michelle and Ray, would be arriving. It was the second anniversary of our annual pilgrimage to the Arlington Cemetery, located just down the street from my house. We had a certain grave to visit. Like the year before, the weather was cold and the ground was covered with a thin blanket of snow.

After my rapid shoveling, the sidewalk was clear, just in time to see Michelle and Ray pulling up to the curb in front of the house. The street was cleared by the town's plows, so there was no need to take my 4 x 4. We did not want to lose Ray's parking spot in front of the house, so we walked the half block to the cemetery. As we crossed Schuyler Avenue, we saw that the large, black gates of the cemetery were open. We walked single file past the gate, with me leading the procession. About fifty feet in, we turned right and walked down the hill on concrete stairs, now covered with virgin snow, that were dug into the hillside. About ten steps down, we stepped off the stairs and approached the gravesite of Daisy Whittle. She was not a relative and had been dead a long time before I arrived on the planet, yet I felt a special kinship with her.

The Christmas wreath that Michelle had placed on the grave earlier in the week still looked fresh, and the light covering of snow gave it a holiday flair. There were no signs of visitors this morning, but in the distance we could see cemetery workers with a pay loader refilling an open grave.

Unlike many cemeteries I have visited, this one has an unusually large number of trees in it. In the winter, when all the leaves are gone, you can get a clear view of midtown Manhattan. The three of us stood solemnly at the grave. All of us had red noses and a hint of smoky-looking breath condensation coming from our mouths as we exhaled, for the temperature was in the low twenties.

Ray walked away from the grave shortly after we arrived. I turned to look at him and saw him lighting a cigarette. It was obvious that Ray thought this pilgrimage was a waste—seriously cutting into his TV time—but to keep peace with Michelle, he would go through our annual routine.

Michelle and I remained standing side by side, staring at the headstone as if we were expecting a personal greeting from our deceased friend. Glancing up, I saw the sun peeking out from behind gray clouds above us. I had no regrets about the trek to this gravesite or holding this annual vigil, because attention to the deceased was long overdue.

The beginning of this story goes back a few years earlier, to when I first met Michelle and her family, and in turn, Daisy.

Daisy Whittle was born in 1886 and died in 1928, and if you haven't pieced it together yet, Daisy Whittle was a ghost.

My involvement with Daisy started in 2007, when a local Jersey City newspaper, *The Jersey Journal*, wanted to write a story about me and my psychic abilities. They had read a story about me in *The Observer*, a newspaper in my hometown of Kearny, New Jersey, and wanted to follow up with their own story. On a Monday afternoon, a college student reporter came to my house to interview me. She sat on my couch and asked the usual questions, such as, "When did you first realize you had this ability?" and "What is life like for a person who has this gift?" Then, near the end of the interview, she put her pen down and asked, "What can you tell me about *me*?"

People do this to me all the time and, honestly, I don't like it. What happens if I tell them something they do not want to hear? Then I suddenly become a monster. With this reporter, I "saw" nothing bad, so after a few seconds I said:

"Every day you come home and put your key into a lock that's part of a large wood and glass door. After you open the door, you turn around to take the key out and you look into the street. By the way, the cars are jammed into the parking places and, judging by how narrow the street is, I would say you live in Jersey City. When the door is closed, you then look at the floor, which is covered with small, white octagon tiles, and there is a crack in those tiles that extends the entire length of the hall. You walk to the end of the hall, turn left, and insert a key into a dark wooden door that lets you into your apartment."

The reporter answered, "I've been living in that apartment in Jersey City my entire life. I live with my parents, and you described the doors, tile, and even the crack in the floor perfectly."

After my little show of psychic ability, she slid her pen and pad neatly into her handbag. She thanked me for the interview and my demonstration and said the interview would be published in the next issue of the paper. True to her word, the article appeared in the very next edition, on September 21. It was an excellent article with no inaccuracies, unlike many others that had been written about me in the past. She had even contacted many experts in the field of the paranormal to ask them about me. These experts included Joanne D.S. McMahon, and Rosemary Ellen Guiley, a paranormal researcher and author of dozens of books. Both of these people, who are prominent in their fields, sang my praises, which embarrassed me a little, because I was very unaccustomed to such attention.

The article pointed out the similarities I share with a fictional character, the little boy in the movie, *The Sixth Sense*, which stars Bruce Willis. The little boy in the movie is exactly who I was as a child. He "sees dead people...*all the time*." Many of the spirits asked favors of him or needed him to help them convey messages to the living. The boy was tortured by his ability to communicate with the dead, just as I have been my whole life. Like the boy, it was not until I began to understand my ability that I became "okay" with it.

The paper listed my e-mail address and telephone number where people could reach me, should they have questions about or problems with the paranormal.

I received a few calls the day the paper came out. Some people wanted me to investigate their troubling paranormal situations. Others had questions about the meaning of their dreams; one even wanted me to explain the odd behavior of his dog when it sees his neighbor. What *they* considered matters of life or death just weren't cutting it for me. These were not things that my psychic ability could be of help with.

On the second day, however, I received a call from a woman named Michelle. Michelle lived on the opposite side of my town.

Her tone and sincerity were genuine, and when she said that there was a ghost living in her house, I believed her. A brief phone conversation could often tell me if the person at the other end of the line was genuine or crazy. To Michelle, there was no question about the existence of this ghost. It was her attitude that made me very curious.

In the past, I had been approached by people claiming to have ghosts in their homes, only to discover, after hours of investigative work, that the constant banging of the steam pipes was nothing more than air trapped in the pipes, or that the curtains and shades that blew wildly and terrified the family were merely drafty windows that needed to be re-caulked.

At the end of my phone conversation with Michelle, I knew that she—and her ghost—were the real deal. We set the time for my visit on the following day.

The next day, knowing that I was about to walk into a situation where I might encounter Michelle's resident ghost, I refrained from eating. If I eat before an investigation where there is some genuine paranormal activity, my stomach gets upset and I feel like vomiting.

The "Daisy house"

The trip from my house to Michelle's took only a few minutes. At the time, I had no idea where on Belgrove Street Michelle's house was located. For most of its length, Belgrove is lined with the town's finest homes. Where the street gets closer to the town of East Newark, the homes lose their driveways, and the buildings become much closer together, some with just a few feet separating them. As the house numbers got closer to Michelle's, the sprawling lawns disappeared and were replaced with steps of concrete and brick. Michelle lived on this part of Belgrove Street.

Her house did not meet most people's expectations of what a haunted house should look like. It was not a sprawling Victorian home with gables, dark shutters, and a horseshoe driveway, like the beautiful homes at the other end of street. This house was a non-descript, three-story building with light yellow aluminum siding. Steep wooden stairs extended two stories to the front door. At street level was a door that led to the basement. Only an alley on each side separated their house from that of their neighbors.

At the base of the stairway was a walled-in area that seemed to be an attempt at a small garden, badly in need of planting and grooming. Michelle was leaning against this garden wall as I drove up. She stood about five feet, six inches tall, and she had short, light-colored hair. As I was crossing the street, she knew immediately that I was the psychic she was waiting for. After our hello's, she ushered me through the lower basement door. She watched me closely as I entered and stared into the basement room for just a moment. I caught sight of something but did not react. Then I turned right and climbed the interior staircase to the second floor.

What I had glimpsed in that basement room was a sickly old man who had lived there recently. It was not a ghost, just an imprint left behind in the room. For now, I kept the vision of that imprint to myself.

Sitting at the kitchen table was Michelle's daughter, Debbie, a young woman about twenty years old, who wore a straight pageboy haircut and black-rimmed glasses. Michelle introduced us, and Debbie said in an almost inaudible voice, "Hello." I sensed that she thought this psychic visit was something stupid that her mother wanted, and that she would have no part of it.

The other human residents of the house were Michelle's husband, Ray, and two more daughters, Elizabeth, and Donna, the youngest, who Michelle affectionately called "Dee Dee."

Michelle spoke about the strange things happening in the house: lights turning on and off, odd noises, and glimpses of shadows. She said that most of these activities happened on the second floor.

Debbie just sat at the table, listening to her mother excitedly describe the ghostly events that she and her family were experiencing. Debbie made it clear that she thought these things were all in her mother's mind, and that she did not think there was a ghost in the house. What I sensed was that Debbie did not want to be considered a person who believed in ghosts. Her fear was that if word got out that she believed her house was haunted, her peers would make fun of her. To a young person, that would be a fate worse than death. It would make her look foolish and "un-cool."

Michelle had about thirty cats living in the house, along with a few dogs. To others, that might make her appear to be eccentric. The scenario of all these pets living in a supposedly haunted house brought to mind something I had read in *The Trickster*, a book written by paranormal researcher George Hansen. To paraphrase Hansen, if a ghost wants to make itself known, it will appear to people who are considered to be eccentric. Should they tell anyone that their house is haunted, people will probably not take it seriously, so ghosts or "entities" can do what they want with no worries of consequences. According to Hansen, spirits actually "choose" the people they haunt, with deliberate attention to how "safe" they will be.

I *like* cats, and was by no means put off by Michelle's desire to keep so many. After taking some time to pet the few cats that walked up to me, I felt it was time to start this investigation. The faster I got through this, the sooner I could eat. I was *very* hungry.

"So, let's start on the second floor," I said.

Michelle answered, "Debbie will take you upstairs, I'll wait here." Michelle looked scared, as though she did not want to go to the second floor. It was obvious that she was nervous about what I would uncover. In her heart, she knew who the specter was and why it was trying to make itself known to her.

I walked through the kitchen and dining room and then made the turn up the stairway. Debbie followed one step behind me. Each stair was fitted with laminate flooring and a squeak came from every second or third stair we stepped on. When I put both feet on the second floor landing and took a few steps forward, I turned my head to look into the bedroom to the right. This was Michelle and Ray's bedroom which, according to Michelle, seemed to be the center of all the ghostly disturbances. Sitting next to the window was the image of a woman.

Michelle was right, and there was no question about it. I was looking at a ghost.

She was wearing wire-rimmed glasses, and her dark, curly hair almost touched her shoulders. A large, Victorian birdcage was to her right, and a brown bird perched on the swing inside. Seeing this image, I froze. The bird was a ghost, too. The only sound I heard from the room was the chirping of the little brown bird in the cage. Just when I thought the image would fade out, this woman turned her head and looked directly at me. The words that came out of her mouth were clear and direct.

"My name is Daisy. I'm in love with a man in New York State, but I'm stuck here in Kearny."

The fact that a ghost was conversing with me did not bother me at all. Daisy's image was sharp and I felt that she was relieved to finally be able to talk to someone who could hear and see her. Her voice was strong, not whispery, and she made it clear that she had something important to say.

Daisy's talking turned into a rant. Her first concern was with the structural changes Michelle and Ray had made to the bedroom. She did not like a wall they had added, because it sliced the room in half. She apparently did not know that the new wall was part of a bathroom they had installed on the second floor.

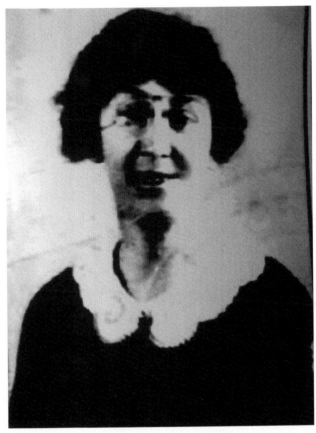

Daisy Whittle's passport photo

While Daisy was speaking her mind to me, the small bird was flying wildly around in the cage, chirping loudly. As Daisy spoke, I didn't say a word. I just listened. I was trying to memorize all the things Daisy had to say so I could repeat them accurately to Michelle and her family. I was sure Debbie was wondering why I was just staring into an empty bedroom, listening intently to "nothing."

If I had spoken to Daisy, would she have heard me? Unfortunately, we will never know. She spoke so quickly that the conversation was one-sided. Daisy had a lot to say and wanted to get it off her chest quickly. I had never before had a spirit engage me in such a detailed conversation. As she spoke, my eyes were fixed on hers, and her eyes stared back at me through her wire-rimmed glasses.

It's a strange thing to look into the eyes of the dead: their eyes do not fully focus on the living. They do not look straight at someone, but a little to the side. Could it be that they see a living person as a blur rather than a clearly fixed image? These questions occurred to me after Daisy was done "unloading" on me. There was no other conscious thought in my head as she went on and on.

Oddly, Daisy's tirade took little more than a minute, but it was a minute filled with her rapid speech. When she was done, her image dissolved and faded away.

Debbie said, "Aren't we going to look around?"

I smiled and said, "I already know about the ghost. We can go downstairs now."

How strange this must have seemed to Debbie! I could almost hear her mother asking her, after I had left, "What did you see?" Debbie would say, "Nothing! I don't know what that psychic guy saw, but I saw absolutely nothing!"

Probably the only thing she *did* see was the blank look on my face as I stood staring into the empty bedroom.

When we walked into the kitchen, Michelle was leaning on the stove. "Well?" she asked impatiently. "Do I have a ghost? And if I do, what's his name?"

I answered, "You *do* have a ghost, and the ghost's name is *Daisy.*"

Michelle straightened up and yelled, "Daisy!" She then spun around to Debbie and screamed, "Did you tell him about the letters?"

Debbie replied, "*What* letters?"

Michelle took off through the kitchen and yelled to both of us, "Wait there!"

Less than a minute later, she returned with a stack of letters wrapped with a yellow bow.

"Here! Look at these!" she said to me, handing me the bundle.

I held in my hands a stack of letters addressed to Daisy Whittle, from Jim Gates of Ballston Spa, New York. Ballston Spa is a town outside of Albany, New York. The postmarks and dates on the letters were from 1920 and 1921. One thing was certain: Daisy had given me accurate information. Her love interest, living in upstate New York, was Jim Gates.

The Daisy love letters (photo altered to remove street address)

I asked Michelle where these letters had come from. Michelle replied in a shaky voice, "They were stuck in the second floor ceiling beams. We found them when we were replacing the plaster ceiling with sheet rock."

Michelle was in shock. About a half hour later, she told me that her father had died just a few weeks before. I knew then that he was the imprint I had seen in the basement room when I had entered the house. Michelle had thought for sure that it was her father who had been haunting the house, and she had wanted to see if I would confirm her suspicion. With this new information regarding Daisy, Michelle's thought of her father being the ghost was forgotten. With Daisy identified as the spirit, there were still many questions that had to be answered, starting with, *who was Daisy?* Why was she haunting this house? What did she want? What should we do next?

I explained to Michelle that this is the real world, not like the ghost hunter programs she had seen on television. The answers to the many questions we had about Daisy would not be answered as quickly as they would be in an hour-long TV show. I was willing to take on this haunting mystery, but it would take time, and it was up to Michelle and her family to have the patience to see this thing through with me to the end.

Michelle agreed, but I did not know how the rest of the family would feel. It would be like a huge jigsaw puzzle: we would examine one piece at a time, always trying to make the pieces fit, so that in the end, we would know the story of Daisy and the reason for her haunting.

The letters were a good start. They gave us an overview of the relationship between Jim Gates and Daisy. He was a store manager of E.C. Welch & Co., of Ballston Spa, NY, "Specializing in Dry Goods, Garments and Millinery," which was boldly printed on a few of the envelopes he had sent to Daisy. Reading his letters gave us a personal profile of Mr. Gates. One function of his job was traveling for the company, and that was probably how he met Daisy. Back home, he was also a fireman in the town's volunteer fire department.

Jim Gates

From time to time, he mentioned the fires he and his fire company were called to put out. He had a love for the Ford automobile that belonged to the company, which he was occasionally allowed access to for his personal use. He would always clean this Model T before and after he used it. The roads in the area were mostly unpaved, and mud often covered the car. Trying to keep it clean was a never-ending battle.

The frequency of these letters sent to Daisy was every few days. When he missed a day, he would apologize in the next letter. By the way, the cost of postage back in 1920 was a whopping two cents.

The personal content of the letters suggested a love relationship between Jim and Daisy. A typical letter, such as the one from February 7, 1921 sent from Jim to Daisy, ended with, "With lots of love I am as ever Jim XXXXXXXXXXXXXXX S W A K." SWAK was shorthand for Sealed With A Kiss. Although Jim's letters were pages long, they did not answer all of the questions I had.

From time to time I visited Michelle to work on the mystery of Daisy. We e-mailed each other often, sometimes many times daily. Michelle said the hauntings were increasing. Could it be that Daisy knew what we were doing and was getting impatient? Was it possible that Daisy could actually be reading the e-mails we exchanged?

We decided to check the phonebook listings around Albany, looking for anyone who could possibly be a family member of Jim Gates. In the flood of calls we made to the Ballston Spa area, we asked those who answered their phones if they had ever heard of a Jim Gates or a Daisy Gates in their families' histories. To our surprise, there were many Gates families still living in the Ballston Spa area. Michelle and I called every one of the Gates families listed, but no one knew of a Jim Gates or of Daisy. The road to finding answers that way reached a dead end.

According to the letters, in early 1921, Jim started writing about a woman named Pearl. I could tell Daisy did not like her, because in his following letter, he tried to explain that he and Pearl were just friends (yes, men used that same line even back in the 1920s!). Then the letters to Daisy abruptly ended. This was probably the time at which the relationship between Jim and Daisy ended. Michelle and I came to the conclusion that there was a strong possibility that Jim Gates was a married man at the time he was involved with Daisy, or his relationship with Pearl became serious. Either scenario left Daisy out of the picture. That would explain the abrupt ending to their correspondence.

We did not have to wait long before something unusual happened. About this time, I was in charge of running a themed party for my Masonic Club. The theme was the 1960s, and I was hard at work with the decorations. To get the people in the sixties mood, I placed two female mannequins, dressed in psychedelic gear, by the front door where the guests came in. I managed to get the proper clothing needed, which included white go-go boots, colorful mini-skirts, and brightly colored headbands. On this particular day, I had one mannequin lying on my living room couch, and I was struggling to put an arm through the sleeve of a dress. Suddenly, at the height of my mannequin-dressing fiasco, Daisy's voice came to me.

Speaking not audibly, but mentally, I heard Daisy ask, "Do you want to see my grave?"

I quickly answered out loud, "Yes!"

Seconds later, the voice returned and told me that if I went to the cemetery located at the foot of the street, I would find it there.

I put on my shoes and began a quick walk, almost a run, to the cemetery. About fifty feet beyond the gates, something told me to turn right and to start looking at the large gravestones. Eight rows down stood a huge family plot with a stone marked, "Whittle." This entire section of the cemetery was on the side of a hill. Sure, there was a gravestone with the name Whittle, but was Daisy buried here? It was just one large stone with no individual names. I was disappointed that neither Daisy's name nor that of any other member of the Whittle family was engraved on the stone.

I decided I would return to the cemetery the next day and visit the cemetery office to check their records to see who was buried in the Whittle family plot. As I was leaving, I saw a small protrusion of a stone just peeking out of the ground. Daisy's voice said to me— commanded me— "Don't leave. *Look* at it."

The stone was deep in the dirt and, of course, I had no shovel with me, so I used the heel of my shoe to kick the dirt away from the stone. Slowly, the dirt revealed a flat gravestone lying beneath. Letter by letter, I poked through the dirt with the heel of my shoe and uncovered the name DAISY and the years of her life, 1886 to 1928.

Daisy had successfully brought me to her grave. I immediately pulled out my cell phone and called Michelle.

"Michelle, I found Daisy's grave!"

Michelle shouted, "How did you find it?"

Without missing a beat, I answered, "Daisy showed me!"

The grave of Daisy Whittle

Daisy's story could not be kept a secret. Michelle's neighbors found out about it, and the town newspaper ran a story about it. Pieces of the puzzle were starting to fit. We found ancestry records on the internet, and phone directories from the 1920s that contributed to our progress. Michelle found Daisy's passport picture on the internet, enlarged the picture and framed it, placing it on a first floor wall next to a framed picture of Daisy's gravestone. Michelle spent hour after hour on the internet, trying to piece together the life and death of Daisy, as well as the Whittle family history.

The weeks flew by as Michelle dug out more information. The gains did not come without costs, however. Michelle's family gave her problems. Debbie and Elizabeth were especially unhappy with their mother's sudden obsession with Daisy. The girls openly insulted their mother because of *"this 'Daisy' thing."* To them, their mother was losing touch with reality by dwelling on a dead woman. Michelle brushed off their insults and continued her research.

People in the neighborhood started joking about the supposed ghost in Michelle's home. As word began to spread, even Michelle's sisters began to question her sanity.

I knew Michelle was being treated unfairly. The ghost was real. Not only did Michelle and I know it, but we also had the proof of the documentation.

Michelle's family's displeasure continued. Even when her daughters witnessed the ghostly goings on, they would deny the incidents and the existence of the ghost rather than bear the taunts and jokes of others. Michelle and I were alone in our curiosity about Daisy Whittle, and it was now up to us to find out why Daisy's spirit had stayed in the house after she had died.

We tried a different approach when my friend, Rosemary Ellen Guiley, who had been quoted in the *Jersey Journal* article about me, came to visit me. She brought something called "Frank's Box," also known as a ghost box, a very strange device. This was a "talk to the dead machine" invented by a man named Frank Sumption. The "box" was a radio scan device that moved rapidly up and down the AM band. The jumble of noise generated as it passed over every radio station within range created a sound background that supposedly enhanced the ability of spirits, including the dead, to talk in real time. The operator asked questions, and sometimes audible answers emerged from the scan. Most answers were short, one to several words.

Ghost boxes were, and still are, controversial in their ability to produce evidence. They have been around in various forms for nearly a century. Many investigators, including Rosemary, have captured mystery voices that are difficult to explain naturally and are not words and phrases generated by the radio stations.

Although I don't use devices like this for my investigations, I welcomed Rosemary to try this device at Michelle's house. Let's face it: we had nothing to lose and it was worth a try, so off we went to Michelle's to test "Frank's Box."

We placed the box on the bed in Michelle's bedroom. Rosemary sat on one side of the bed and I sat opposite her. I had brought along a fellow Freemason from my lodge named Jim Battista, who had always wanted to be part of a ghost investigation. Jim had begged me a number of times to join me on this ghost venture, and the presence of such a celebrity as Rosemary made it extra special. I always have reservations about bringing an outside person to an investigation, but knowing Jim as well as I did, I finally agreed. I instructed him to be quiet as we tried out this experiment with "the box." He stood quietly at the foot of the bed, not saying a word or making a move.

We turned on the machine and turned up the volume.

Knowing about the birdcage I had seen next to Daisy, Rosemary asked, "What is the name of your bird?"

"Chocolate," a voice from the box answered.

"Do you have a dog?"

A reply came quickly, "Chestnut."

It seemed we were having luck with questions pertaining to pets, so Rosemary asked, "Do you have any cats?"

In a loud voice, we heard "CATS!"

Well, it didn't take a genius to get the message that, if this was Daisy, she did not like cats. I am sure she would see cats as a threat to her bird, "Chocolate." Daisy was probably quite agitated about all of Michelle's cats in the house.

As we were addressing our questions to "the box," Jim felt something brush across his leg. He thought it was one of Michelle's cats, but then realized that the room was cat-free. Although this made him uneasy, he was a real trooper. Jim continued to watch in complete silence.

Suddenly, as if someone or something had come in between Rosemary and me, what felt like a hand pushed us both nearly off the bed. Jim watched this happen. As we recovered from this show of force, I looked up at Jim, who had a look of fright on his face. He looked back at me and said, "I think I just soiled myself!"

We tried again to regain contact with our spirit but could not. Was this a spirit communicating with us, or was it a coincidence that these words just happened to come out of an AM radio band? There is no way to be certain. In any case, it was an interesting experiment. I resolved, however, to continue relying upon my own psychic impressions.

As time passed from one month to the next, I received many calls from Michelle telling me about disturbing dreams she was having. Michelle felt as if Daisy was trying to tell her about the terrible life she had led living in this house with her family.

Dreams about Daisy were not limited to Michelle; images of Daisy's life made their way into my dreams, night after night, as well. I could feel the anxiety Daisy felt living in that house. In these images, I could see through her eyes, viewing her streetas it looked in the 1920s. Nostalgic visions of the1920s gave way to feelings of abuse, both mental and physical, perpetrated on her by her father and by others. Sometimes I would see her as a young girl, then at other times I would see a much older Daisy. Michelle's dreams were very similar to mine, but I kept my "Daisy dreams" from Michelle. I did not want to influence what Michelle was experiencing by sharing my visions and dreams with her.

Dream influences from the dead and spirits is a phenomenon in many hauntings. The ability of the discarnate to invade the dreams of the living has been known and documented since ancient times. It may be easier to connect with the living when we are asleep and the busy waking consciousness is out of the way. It is always important, in any paranormal investigation, to ask about unusual dreams.

In time, all the pieces started to fit. The census of the 1920s showed that Daisy's house back then was always full of family and relatives. The passport records revealed that her father made frequent trips to England, and he always came back with another male family member. These new additions stayed with the family for a year or two, and then they would mysteriously disappear. It appears that Mr.

Whittle had found a way to beat the immigration quota system. He always brought a baby back with him, declaring it as his son.

We also uncovered that, for additional income, the Whittles would take in boarders. But how did all this affect Daisy? Was she a slave to her father and forced to take care of these boarders? Who fed and cleaned up after them? There was an older sister named Ada, but she was never a factor in this haunting.

As Daisy got older, she never left home. We did know that seven years before she died, Daisy had a personal and romantic relationship with Jim Gates, but it ended abruptly. Both Michelle and I felt that there was another woman who entered Jim Gates's life—or perhaps her relationship with Jim Gates interfered with her duties at home. Perhaps her father feared she would marry and leave him. Daisy told me that she was "stuck" in Kearny. Why? Could it be the boarder scenario I described, or perhaps a health issue with her father? Why didn't Ada help? How about the others in the family? There were still many unanswered questions to the Daisy riddle.

The question that people ask today is, if things were that tough for Daisy, why didn't she just pack up and leave? We must remember the time frame. In Daisy's time, women had few rights. They had to deal with prejudice in the workplace, such as earning lower wages than men did. Very few job opportunities were open to them and these were mostly for young, single women. It was not until the passing of the Nineteenth Amendment to the U.S. Constitution in 1920 that women were granted the right to vote. Although it was a huge milestone for women's rights, women were still considered second-class citizens. Without money or connections, a woman like Daisy could easily become destitute if she left home to try to make it on her own, because most of our social "safety net" systems were non-existent then.

With the information we uncovered, Michelle and I came to the same conclusion. Although we cannot substantiate it, we believe Daisy was the victim of cruelty by her family members and boarders, and was subjected to mental, physical, and sexual abuse. To this day, those horrid acts of cruelty against Daisy still surface through visions that come to me from time to time. In Jim Gates, she may have seen a savior who would rescue her from her plight. It must have been a bitter, heart-crushing disappointment when that relationship abruptly ended.

Daisy's life ended in her forty-second year. She died in 1928 of lumbar pneumonia, according to her death certificate. She was buried on a cold day in December and, according to the records, her family did not even provide a casket for her. Her body was wrapped in a blanket and lowered into the ground with rope.

The reason for the haunting was clear to me. Daisy's existence was ignored in the house full of family and boarders. All the attention was given to the men, not to Daisy. Daisy wanted love and acknowledgement, but she received neither. Daisy was haunting this house because she wanted people to know that she once existed, and she hated the fact that she had been forgotten.

What Michelle did next was great—a textbook perfect way to deal with a spirit who wants the world to know of her existence.

Daisy's birthday was in August, so Michelle decided to throw a birthday party for her. She ordered a cake and placed birthday candles on the cake with the big numbers 4 and 3. We wanted this to be a celebration of Daisy's forty-third birthday: the birthday she never had.

Out came the grill, salads, burgers, hot dogs, and assorted munchies. I invited my friend Josh and his girlfriend Ary. My friend Christine Hague came with her husband Mark. I was there with Sueli, my wife. Joining Michelle and Ray were their three daughters and two of Michelle's close friends. All these people joined in celebrating Daisy's birthday.

Michelle's yard is typical of what you would find in this town. A large above-ground pool took up most of the yard, and a high cyclone fence flanked both sides of the property. The party took place on the small patio between the kitchen and the pool. Michelle went all out and got silver Mylar helium balloons with the words "Happy Birthday" printed on them in bright blue and red. The balloons were tied to the tables and fences. They swayed and bobbed as the wind constantly whipped around the house. We ate, drank, and had a wonderful time, and toasted the birthday girl. Sadly, only the birthday girl was missing from the festivities. Of course, if anyone outside the sphere of Michelle's family and friends had known the real purpose of this party, they would have been convinced that we were all crazy. But *this* party, planned by Michelle, paid off.

Toward the end of the afternoon, I had a feeling that I should return to the second floor bedroom, and that Daisy would be there. I looked at Christine and asked if she would join me to see if Daisy would show. Michelle was not happy. I could tell she was hurt that I did not ask her to accompany us, but I had my reasons. Michelle had a high-strung personality. I knew she would make comments and ask questions as I was trying to concentrate, so asking her to join us would have been disastrous.

Christine and I left the party and went upstairs. Once in the bedroom, I called Daisy's name. Christine was seated on the side of the bed, and it was obvious that she was a bit nervous. A few minutes later, I saw Daisy walk into the room through the closed door. Before I could utter a word, Christine told me that her entire right side was numb and cold. Daisy was now entirely in the room and standing next to Christine's right side. I called out to Daisy, but she just stared straight ahead.

Daisy said, "Bells! Bells! I love the sound of the bells. They played them at my funeral." She continued, "The beautiful songs of the bells." She gave a slight smile, and walked past Christine and upward, as if she were walking up a ramp. Then she passed through the wall. Daisy was gone.

The cold and numb sensation lifted from Christine's body. Immediately I felt a heaviness lift from the room and from my mind. Right before my eyes, Daisy had "crossed over" to the other side. She was free.

We returned to the party. I explained what had happened to Christine and that Daisy had crossed over to the afterlife. Michelle was very upset.

She shouted, "I wanted to go upstairs to see Daisy! Why didn't you ask *me* to go?" I did not want to hurt her by explaining why I had not done that. I tried to answer her by simply saying, "You're too close to the situation."

After all the time we had invested in this case and all the research we had done, and all the emotional and mental pain we had shared with Daisy, it was now over. But there was still something about what Daisy had said before she crossed over that bothered me. It was Daisy's reference to "the bells." What were the bells she spoke of?

Daisy's final words stayed with me for days and bothered me. It was the last piece of the puzzle but I could not fit it into the picture. I decided to retrace my steps to see if I had overlooked something important. I called Michelle and asked her to remind me of exactly when Daisy had died.

"December 27th," she replied.

Immediately, the mystery of the bells was solved. Just a few blocks from Daisy's home is a Catholic church that was part of an orphanage for boys called Boystown.

Back in the 1920s, some of the orphaned boys were taught to play songs by ringing the bells in the church steeple. They performed these songs at Christmastime, nightly from December 20 to January 6. *These* were the beautiful bells Daisy described. I guess we will never know what song was playing as Daisy drew her last breath, but it must have been lovely.

There is a final, eerie note regarding this haunting. Michelle tracked down the previous owner of her house. His telephone number was listed, so she gave him a call.

"Did anything strange ever happen while you lived in this house, like the lights going on and off, or doors opening and closing by themselves?" she asked.

He told Michelle that he was a truck driver. When he had lived in the house, he always left early in the morning and came home late at night. He only ate and slept there. He said he had lived there with his mother, who suffered from Alzheimer's disease.

"She was never quite right," he told Michelle. "When I came home from work, I would always ask her how her day went. She always told me that early every morning, she had tea with someone named *Daisy*. Seems she was *always* having tea with *Daisy*. I checked with the woman who was watching her for me and a few of the neighbors, and no one knew anybody named Daisy, so it must have been all in her mind."

To this day, I still visit Daisy's grave. It gives me a chance to clean off Daisy's gravestone, otherwise dirt will cover it. When I stand over the grave, the ambient sounds of the present disappear and psychic images flash back to the burial in 1928. Close to the grave I can see the faces of six family members, while a handful of others stand motionless behind the gravestones surrounding her grave. What stays with me is the pronounced uncaring look on the minister's face as he reads from his prayer book. It is New Year's Eve, which created the perfect excuse for many people to avoid the funeral and burial. There are only a few flowers placed on the green blanket that hides the dirt pile of the grave.

The scene reminded me of the Beatles' song, *Eleanor Rigby*, about "all the lonely people."

As I stand by Daisy's grave on my annual visits, those images of the past come and then fade away, and I am back in today's world. I know that it is time for me to leave, and I slowly walk back to my parked truck. As I pause by the front gate of the cemetery on Schuyler Avenue, I see car after car pass by and wonder how many Model A's and T's passed by this very gate back in 1928, the day they buried Daisy.

Daisy finally received the recognition she always wanted, not from her contemporaries, but eighty years later, from people born long after she died. This experience will stay with me for the rest of my life.

Thank you, Daisy, for sharing your life with us, and now may you rest in peace.

3

From Daydreams to Nightmares

Many researchers and parapsychologists say that psychics are created as a result of their environments and family histories. To understand why I have the abilities that I do, I had to take a closer look at my early life, and how my experiences made me different.

Compared to the rest of my family, I was certainly the odd one. I enjoyed music, films, and art. Those qualities were not considered practical or beneficial in my family. My grandfather, Alexander Pietrzykowski, came to the United States from Poland at the turn of the twentieth century. He, along with other men from Eastern Europe, eagerly took the offer this country made to them: "Free passage to the United States if you become a coal miner."

A miner's life was not an easy one, but it was a better one than he had in Poland. Alexander had served as a sailor in the Russian navy and had fought in the Russo-Japanese War. Although he'd had three ships sink under him, he had miraculously managed to survive.

He left Europe behind and began his new life's adventure in Northeast Pennsylvania, living the life of a coal miner. Free from European wars, he must have felt like he had arrived in the Promised Land.

In reality, life for a miner back then was hard and dangerous, and the life expectancy was short. Maybe that was why miners like my grandfather produced so many children. Boys would provide additional income for the household, and girls would help their mothers with housework. Later, the boys would also work in the mines, marry, and continue the cycle of bearing many children. My father, Walter, was one of eight children, and he and his siblings did not have an easy life, either. Alexander was strict, and the slightest infraction would often be answered with a cat-o-nine tails whip to their backs.

Karl's family members, from left: Grandmother Veronica, Grandfather Alexander, Aunts Jenny and Josephine, Cousin John, Uncle Peter with Jenny's daughter Patricia. Circa 1942.

I know very little about my grandmother. As I was growing up, no one talked about her. Even the mention of her name was taboo in our house. Later, I found out why.

My father and his brothers were all veterans of World War II, and all made it back home safely. This was apparently not welcome news to my grandmother. One day, while my father was lying on the couch in the parlor, he overheard a conversation between his mother and aunt.

"With all my sons in the war, you would think at least one of them would have been killed, so I could get money from the government," his mother complained.

His aunt was shocked to hear this comment from her sister, and she insisted that my grandmother did not mean what she had said, but my grandmother did not retract her comment—because she had meant it. For my father, those words coming out of his mother's mouth hurt him terribly. The great love a son has for his mother is often talked about, but in this case, his mother returned that love by wishing him or one of his brothers dead. What kind of mother would trade any of her son's lives for a fistful of money?

Shortly after hearing those words, my father walked out of the house with just the clothes on his back and left Pennsylvania to start his life over, this time in New Jersey. His older sister, Emily, was married to a man named Chester and living in Newark, so my Dad, with nowhere else to go, hitchhiked to Newark with only ten cents in his pocket and the hope of temporarily living with Emily and Chester until he could get on his feet.

Newark is a large city, and my father, Walter, had no idea where in Newark they lived. What made matters worse was that he did not even know his sister's married name. The last driver that gave Walter a lift dropped him off in Newark on Lafayette Street, which was in a neighborhood near the airport. Luck was on my father's side that day. He began his search by walking the street, asking people if they knew where Chester and Emily lived. He went door to door until someone said he knew them, and that they lived at 98 Pulaski Street, which was only four city blocks from where he had been dropped off.

The houses in Newark were different from the ones in his hometown of Larksville, Pennsylvania. No picket fences, porches, or porch swings. With the exception of a few houses, all the buildings on the street were made of brick. My father walked down Pulaski Street past the houses, bars, and stores and, just past St. Casimir's Polish Catholic Church and school, he reached number 98. His final destination was a three-story brick building with a shoemaker's shop in the basement. Only a foot of space separated this building from the next one. He entered the dimly-lit hall and went up the stairs to the second floor apartment, where Emily answered his knock.

She was happy to see him and very surprised. No one from the family had ever ventured a trip to see her since she had gotten married. Walter was very hungry; he had not eaten since he had left Pennsylvania. He had only half a pack of cigarettes remaining from the full one that the last driver had given him during his trip. Emily quickly fixed a sandwich for him. This would hold him over until she made dinner, which would be ready just about the time Chester arrived home from his job at the Esso refinery.

Lottie Helinski Petry   *Walter Petry*

It must have been hard to sit down with his sister and brother-in-law and give them the reason why he had left home and come to New Jersey. They were both shocked and sympathetic as he told his story. That night, a place was set for him in their small apartment. This was day one of my father's new life.

Soon after his arrival, Walter met Lottie Helinski. She was literally the girl next door, living at 100 Pulaski Street. Her life had not been a bed of roses, either. Shortly after Lottie was born, her mother (my maternal grandmother), Karolina, died from complications of childbirth. Honoring a deathbed request, Karolina's sister, Josephine, took Lottie in and raised her. Unfortunately, Lottie's father—my grandfather—abandoned the family soon after Karolina died. Lottie's older siblings, Eleanor, Ted, Wally, and Tony, were taken to a Catholic orphanage in Lodi about ten miles from Newark.

The commonality of difficult childhoods and growing up with the Polish heritage brought my parents together. Walter and Lottie married in 1948 and settled in the same neighborhood in Newark. They lived in the Ironbound section: the name stemmed from the three railroad lines that enclosed the community. It was a small enclave of working class people, many of whom were of Polish descent. These first generation Americans felt a sense of comfort in an area where the local church and school offered classes taught in Polish, the pork store made its own kielbasa, and their neighbors were much like themselves. Their lives were better than their parents' had been, and they hoped for something even better for their children. It was a tough but honest existence.

That, in a nutshell, is the environment in which I grew up. Though television shows portray American life in the 1950s as carefree, our lives were quite the opposite. Small, cold-water flats, with the basics for furnishings and only a toilet in the bathroom, were commonplace.

I would on, occasion, accompany my father to the neighborhood bathhouse, where, for ten cents, we each were given a small bar of soap and a towel. Ironbound Newark had many factories and foundries, and very few of the workers' apartments had showers or bathtubs, so they would stop by the bathhouse to clean up before going home. The bathhouse was an enormous building on Wilson Avenue. The stairs leading to the main floor were huge; it was like entering a big city courthouse. The vestibule was equally immense. The windows were two stories tall! In the corner was the cashier, sitting in what looked like a movie theater ticket booth, with piles of white towels behind him and small bars of Ivory soap at arm's reach.

After my father and I got our towels and soap, it was off to the changing room, then naked to the showers. As a young boy, I felt very strange to have naked men in shower stalls all around me. I can remember being the only child there, and it gave me a squeamish feeling. There was also a swimming pool in this bathhouse but, like the showers, the pool policy stated that no bathing suits were allowed. Looking at some of the naked characters swimming in the pool made any thought of joining them out of the question.

Aside from the bathhouse, there was the option of bathing at home in a zinc tub my father had bought at an Army Navy surplus store downtown. When it was bath time, we'd slide out the tub that was stored under my bed and place it in the middle of the kitchen floor. Pots of water were heated on the stove, and then a mix of hot and cold water was poured into the tub until it was ready for my mother's bath. After my mother, then it was my father's turn. By the end of his bath, the water was cold and dirty, so the tub was emptied, and the routine of filling it began again. This time, my brother was first, then me.

With the apartments crammed closely together, you had little choice but to be close to your neighbors. We could smell what they were having for dinner and, although the walls were thick with plaster and lath, the open windows for ventilation and cooling ensured that we knew not only who was arguing but also what they were arguing about. By today's standards, this seems remarkably primitive, but for us, it was just the way we lived. In short, we were no richer or poorer than our neighbors.

This was a practical existence with no money or time to squander on the trivial pursuits of the arts or music, which I loved. My mother was a great singer and could have had a successful career singing opera. With two children and little money to spare to pay babysitters, her singing was limited to the church choir. The aunt who had raised her, Josephine, once told her to "forget this silly notion of becoming a professional singer. The only singing you'll be doing is singing to your babies."

I didn't mean to be difficult, but somehow my behavior brought out the worst in Dad. Something as inconsequential as not turning off the light when leaving a room would often result in a severe beating. I can vividly remember, after a strapping, my overwhelming desire to escape, to just get away. I knew there was no way I could do so *physically*, so I would remove myself emotionally from the scene. I insulated myself from the torment by withdrawing into myself. I would remain as quiet as I could be and dream of better days to come. My school grades were never good; "too much daydreaming" is what the nuns, or, as we called them, "sisters," termed it.

But were they really daydreams, or were they visions I was seeing? I recall one day in the fourth grade, sitting next to the windows in the classroom. I was looking out of the window and watching as men built the homes across the street. To me, this was in real time, happening now, in 1962, but those houses had been built in the 1920s!

Seeing my distraction, the sister asked me what I was looking at.

"I'm looking at the men building those houses," I answered.

She looked out the window and saw the well-established houses, quietly sitting there with no one working on them. The students in my class laughed, and she quickly belittled me in front of them—the nuns were masters at both mental and physical torment of the little boys and girls in their classes. I soon learned that it was best for me to keep these mental "getaways" to myself, because talking about them often got me into trouble. The nuns frowned on my obvious lack of attention. My parents were upset that I was doing poorly at school. I am certain it was a personal embarrassment for them to have a son who was not a model student. But even so, I continued to lose myself in this other world. The vicious cycle continued: a cycle of punishment for daydreaming, and then daydreaming to escape the pain of punishment from the nuns.

My visions extended beyond school. I recall looking at a Model T Ford coming down Pulaski Street, with a driver who was wearing an odd cap.

I said to my brother, "Hey! Look at that old car!"

He said, "What car?"

"That old car with the guy wearing the hat!" I said.

My brother just made a face at me, which got us into a fight. Of course, there was no car for him to see, but to me, it was as real as one could possibly be.

Mom and Dad hoped to provide my brother, Mark, and me with a decent education, so they did what many other parents did: they sent us to the local parochial school. At St. Casimir's School, the nuns were as strict and sadistic. The "spare-the-rod-spoil-the-child" mentality was as equally important to the nuns as the golden rule. And, I have to say, neither the nuns nor my dad spared the rod. In fact, if Dad found out I had misbehaved at school, he beat me again that night to ensure that I had "learned my lesson."

I believe the nuns found mistreating their students a way to release their frustration of living a celibate life. When a woman became a nun, she received a ring to show she was now one with God. This spiritual union seemed to have little to no impact on the nuns' cruelty to students. It was a common occurrence that, when a student was called to the blackboard and did not know the answer to the question posted on the board, the nun would backhand the student across the face, ring side out, leaving a painful scratch mark on the cheek. The nuns were very good at this. The scratch left a red mark, but seldom bled. We students called it, "the red badge of courage."

Another means of discipline was the pointer. The pointer was a long wooden stick with a rubber tip on it. Poor penmanship or talking during class could get you several whacks with the pointer over your outstretched hands. Once, the nun missed a boy's hand and hit his wrist. The misplaced blow cut the skin and blood squirted into the face of the nun and turned the boy's white uniform shirt into a red polka-dotted mess. An ambulance was called, and the boy's wounds were sewn up. His parents never complained, and he returned to school the next day.

There was a rule for the girls in the class: no patent leather shoes were to be worn. Patent leather was shiny, and the nuns believed the boys could look at the tips of the shoes and see the reflection of the girls' underwear. One day, one of the girls in my class came to school wearing new patent leather shoes. Of course, the girl didn't buy the shoes—her mother did. That morning, when the boys and girls lined up in the hallway to be let into the classroom, Mother Superior walked up to the girl with the new shoes and slapped her hard across the face, sending her to the floor. To this day, I can still see that poor girl crawling on the hall floor, crying uncontrollably, only to hear Mother Superior screaming at her about her shoes.

Punishment was not limited to physical methods. The nuns also dealt out psychological torture. Catholic schools were known for the selling of "chances." One way to make money was to sell chances to win prizes like a television set, food blender, or fifty dollars in cash. Each student was required to take a book of these chances and sell them. Each book had ten. After school, the streets were flooded with kids going from house to house, trying to sell their book or books of chances. It was a poor neighborhood, and the cost of a chance could also buy a loaf of bread, so there were more sellers than buyers. Some parents would take the chance books to work with them, but in many factories, selling their kids' chances was frowned upon. When the day came to turn in the money from the chances, a panic went through the class for all those who dared to return to school with unsold chances. Those who did not sell all their chances were told to line up at the blackboard.

I had to sell not only my book of chances but my brother's, too. My parents always spared my brother the task of door-to-door selling. My brother had a problem with his left leg and selling those chances required the climbing of stairs throughout the neighborhood. It would have been extremely painful, if not impossible for him. When I sold the first book, it was considered my brother's. I still had a few unsold chances in "my" book that now put me in the line with the others at the blackboard. I was in the third grade at the time.

The nuns, in order to teach us a lesson, brought us upstairs to the eighth grade classrooms. An eighth grader, to a kid in third grade, is like an adult. It was scary. The nun had instructed the eighth grade students to laugh at the third grader who was brought, all alone, to the front of the classroom. They would laugh until the third grader was humiliated. Then the next one would be brought in. I was standing in the hall, next to a very nervous boy. He was visibly shaking. I didn't know what to say or do; he was next in line to be humiliated by those big, scary kids. The nun grabbed his arm and led him from the hall, to the room, then to the front of the class. The door to the classroom did not close all the way, and I was able to see him in front of the room. The nun motioned to the class to begin their laughing, but the boy just stood there. He did not cry. He just opened his mouth and twisted his head from the left and to the right, not making any sound. The nun became angry and told the class to laugh more. This brought the boy to his knees, but still with no tears and no sound. Frustrated, the nun grabbed the boy and removed him from the class.

It was now my turn. It wasn't hard to muster tears after seeing what was going on, and shortly after I went in, I was out. I was taught a valuable lesson: that selling those chances should be taken more seriously, especially to a third grader like me.

The poor boy who'd had a breakdown in front of the class never returned to school.

In 1964, I often woke up in the morning spitting up blood. I felt lousy and often was too sick to attend school. After a few trips to the doctor, no cause for my illness could be found.

The doctor finally asked my mother what school I attended. When she answered, "St. Casimir's," he said, "No wonder! Get him out of that school and he'll be fine."

Psychosomatic illnesses were not something many parents believed in. They thought we were just being "sissies." I was not alone, for other students from the school had the same symptoms. I guess the cruelty of the nuns took its toll on the physical well-being of the students. My parents removed me from St. Casimir's School and enrolled me in Ann Street School, the local public school. My illness vanished.

Ann Street was very different from St. Casimir's. Teachers, instead of nuns, taught students, and there was no slapping or hitting students in the classroom as there had been at the Catholic school. This was a great relief to me, as I had never reacted positively to this method of teaching.

I remember my first day at Ann Street. I stood in front of the class and was introduced by the teacher, Miss Ruffolo. I got my first impression of the contrast between my old and new schools as I stood before the class. At Ann Street, the girls and boys were seated next to each other, not segregated by girl rows and boy rows. The kids wore different kinds of clothing, not uniforms, and there were Latinos and even an African American student in class, not just students with Eastern European backgrounds. This was all new and scary to me, but in a short time I welcomed this change in my life.

I was getting psychic signs all the time now, but I could not put them in their proper perspective. For example, I could look at a teacher walking in the hall of the school, and I would know what was on his mind. Once I saw a male teacher was standing near the cafeteria and I knew, just by looking at him, that his girlfriend was one of the pretty blonde teachers in the school. A few minutes later, that very same blonde teacher walked up to him, whispered a few words in his ear, and they both walked away with smiles on their faces. Their relationship came out months later, and was a shock to many of the teachers to learn that they were "an item."

I knew when a "surprise" test was to be given and what shop project the teacher had in mind before he discussed it with the class. Although this sounds like a student's dream, it was not. I thought it was just coincidence or just a string of lucky guesses. I paid it little mind and went on with my day-to-day life.

However, there was one teacher who knew something was different about me. He was the art teacher, Mr. Bernard Zimmer. I do not recall what I initially said to him that piqued his curiosity about me. Before class, he would come to me and ask me questions on various subjects. One example was when he showed me a book with four famous paintings on the page. He asked what I thought of them. I hesitated for a moment, then my impressions kicked in and I answered him. First, I told him what I thought of the paintings, and then I told him what I thought the painter had had in mind when he painted them. Mr. Zimmer walked away with a satisfied look on his face—a bit odd to me at the time—but I was just a kid, and this was all new to me.

One day before class, he asked what I thought about an upcoming teachers' strike and if I thought it would really happen. I answered that the teachers would strike for about a week—this was what the board of education expected of them—and then they would negotiate with the teachers' union and things would get back to normal soon after. It happened just that way, as if they were following my script. Mr. Zimmer was impressed. When we returned to school after the strike, he smiled at me as if to say, "Thanks."

The school had an open house every year, so my parents came to the school to speak to my teachers about how their boy was doing. The last teacher they spoke to was Mr. Zimmer. My parents walked into the classroom and looked at all the displayed artwork done by all the students he taught. They spotted an art project I had done and wanted his opinion about it. It was not my drawing he wanted to talk to them about, though.

When they asked how I was doing, he said, "Karl is different."

My parents thought that he meant artistically, but he said, "That's not what I mean." He insisted, "Karl sees things differently and he's not like the other students in the class." This "feeling" he had about me was foreign to him and he could not put his finger on it. He was not alone. I had that same problem!

Things began looking better for me. Shortly before I changed schools, we moved to what we called a new "modern" apartment, with steam heat, hot water from the tap, and a built-in bathtub. We had a yard with flowers, a place to store our bicycles, and a rat-free basement, which we considered a blessing.

In the old apartment house, the basement had many rats. There were so many that the delicatessen owner, Sidney, who operated the store in our building, complained about them invading his bread deliveries. The bread was delivered and placed in the hall of our apartment house every morning at about 4 AM. Sid opened the store at 6 AM. In those two hours, rats would make their way to the hall from the basement and would gnaw at the bag until they could liberate a roll or two. My father was a good friend of Sid's, and after hearing the about the mysterious case of the vanishing rolls, he personally took on the problem. He got a large box of rat traps, baited them, and placed them in the basement. By the time he walked out of the basement, he could hear the traps going off. He got a garbage can and placed it outside the building. He kept retrieving the sprung traps and dropping the dead rats into the can. An impromptu assembly line was formed: Sidney brought out new traps, I took the bloody, used traps to my mother on the third floor, my mother washed them and dried them, and I brought those traps back to the street, handing them to my father who baited them and placed them back in the basement.

This continued all day until the snap of traps stopped. My father then went into the basement with a flashlight to see where these rats were coming from. In one of the corners was a hole that went directly into the main sewer pipe under the building, home to thousands of rats. As long as that hole existed, rats would have easy access to the basement. My father got cement and bricks and sealed up the hole and the rat problem disappeared.

This was especially good news for the landlord's son, Milton. The landlord was a Polish woman, and Milton was an alcoholic. He drank cheap wine. "Mission Bell" was his wine of choice, as evidenced by the hundreds of empty bottles thrown under the basement stairs. She would not allow him into her apartment, so he was banished to a cot in the basement for sleeping. One cold night, when my father went into the basement to get a can of oil for the kitchen stove, he looked into the coal bin where Milton slept, and saw rats lying on his chest. My father thought that Milton had died and that the rats were eating him! He took the oil can and slammed it on the wall, which scared the rats enough to make them jump off of Milton's chest and run away.

My father approached Milton, expecting the worst, when Milton sat up and said, "They were only trying to keep warm!"

As you may have guessed, my folks expected a lot from me. They wanted me to grow up strong and self-sufficient. In order to do this, they reasoned, I should learn the value of a dollar. So, in addition to my household chores, I worked outside the house, either at the local deli or sorting pipes and fittings at a plumbing contractor's house a few blocks away.

My father was loved in the neighborhood. His generosity was greatly appreciated by our landlord, who lived in the apartment above us. When it snowed, my father would show his kindness by having *me* shovel our sidewalk, as well as the neighbors' sidewalks. In addition, I shoveled the snow from alongside of our house to the yard. Dad became very popular with the neighbors, and I became very strong.

On one particular Saturday in December, I awoke to four inches of wet, slushy snow. I ate my breakfast and started my shoveling. My father reminded me to make sure I shoveled the neighbors' sidewalks. The snow was particularly heavy, and the shoveling was painfully slow. By the time I had finished the front of the house, I was tired, but pushed on. I heard my name being called. It was my Uncle Eddie, who was stopping by to visit my parents. I had always liked Uncle Eddie. He was a pleasant sort and was always kind to me. After he entered the house, I put the shovel to the ground to finish the final ten feet.

As I was about to shovel the last bit of snow, I felt someone watching me. I quickly turned and saw a short, heavyset woman standing only two feet to the side of me, staring at me with a slight smile. It was as if she was happy to see me clearing the sidewalk, yet I could see that this woman was inappropriately dressed for standing in the cold and snow. She wore a hat with a veil (many women's hats had veils attached to them in those days), no coat, a fancy black dress, and she was clutching a large purse in front of her. She looked like the stereotypical Polish woman, so common in our neighborhood. Her sudden appearance, however, startled me. Why was she standing so close to me, and why didn't she say anything? Something was terribly wrong and it scared me.

I screamed, throwing the shovel into the air towards the yard and ran. A few seconds later, I composed myself, and I got angry with this old woman who had scared me. I felt as if she had scared me on purpose, so I grabbed the shovel and decided to confront her. I returned to the spot where I had been shoveling, but she was gone. It had only been a few seconds since I had seen her! Where was she? I went into the house where my mother, father, and uncle were sitting, and asked, "Who was that Polish lady outside?" They did not know what I was talking about.

I ran outside to the front of the house, then to the corner. No Polish lady. She had vanished. I thought she must have had a car sitting in the front with the engine running to get away so quickly. I was still shaken, but within an hour, I put the entire incident behind me. Little did I know that the memory of this incident would surface again, but not until three years later.

My transition from Ann Street School to East Side High School in 1966 was uneventful. The high school was only a block from Ann Street and next door to St. Casimir's School. Almost all of the graduating students from Ann Street went to this school. It was a good school and it was the school my mother graduated from in 1943.

One day, when I was returning home from high school, I found the back kitchen door chained from the inside. This was something we did not do. I pushed the door open as far as the chain would allow, and I saw that our apartment was in shambles. All the cabinets had been emptied and their contents thrown onto the floor. It was clear that our apartment had been broken into and ransacked. I entered the apartment through the front door that had been left open by the burglars. I called my mother at work and told her what had happened. She told me to call the police and leave the house in case someone was still there. The police arrived in a few minutes and went through the apartment, observing and taking notes about the damage.

One of the policemen walked up the hall stairway to the second floor and said that the second floor apartment, the landlord's, had also been broken into. He asked me to join him as he entered the apartment. In all the years that our family had lived in the house, we had never been in our landlord's apartment. The place looked like no one had painted it in decades. The walls and ceiling were a chocolate brown with paint peeling from the ceiling. There were water stains on the ceiling, too—a tell-tail sign that the roof had at one time had a leak. The curtains had probably been white and lacy at one time, but now, like the rest of the apartment, they were brown.

The bottoms of the windows were rotted and falling apart, and I noticed that the curtains would move every time the wind blew outside. The furniture was old, and the apartment gave an overall impression that no one lived there. I got a chilling feeling that our landlord, Joseph Lawsky, had made this apartment a shrine to his mother, and that he had left it untouched after she died. Except for a few dresser drawers from the bedroom, which were lying on the floor, the place had suffered little damage.

In the bedroom, I noticed a picture on the dresser. It was of a short, heavyset old woman, smiling slightly, wearing a fancy black dress, and a hat with a veil. She was clutching a large purse in front of her. It was the Polish lady I had seen three years earlier while I was shoveling snow!

When the landlord came home, he stopped by our apartment for details of what had happened. I told him the whole story, including accompanying the police into his apartment. Before he left, I asked him about the lady in the picture on his dresser. He replied, "That's my mother. She died in 1954."

Thinking back to that snowy day, I know that it was a turning point in my life. The practical boy from a practical home living in a practical world took his first step into a very strange world. I was born into a lineage of coal miners and factory workers, and this ghostly event greatly altered my "practical" world, steering me in a different direction in life. As time went by, I accepted my unusual abilities to see, hear, and feel things others could not.

In the years that followed, it would be parapsychologist Dr. Joanne D.S. McMahon who would put all the pieces together for me and would make sense out of these odd abilities of mine. She would be the first to call me *"The Absent Witness."*

High school was markedly different from Ann Street. Instead of having two teachers for the entire day, we had one for each class. I was on "overload" because it was too much, too fast. It took time to acclimate myself to this new system. New faces came together from various elementary schools in the district. Most of these students came from the East Ward public schools.

East Side High School was different from the schools in the suburbs. A large percentage of students came from homes where English was a second language, and the primary languages were

Portuguese, Spanish, and Polish. Most of the kids entering the school were the sons and daughters of blue-collar workers. Their parents did not take "crap" from their kids and, like my father, did not hesitate to use whatever means were available to make their displeasure known. This was the perfect formula for making bullies out of some kids and overly-passive "targets" out of others.

Unlike a parochial high school that can pick and choose who it accepts, a public school cannot, so teachers gladly got rid of their eighth grade "troublemakers" by allowing them to graduate, whether they deserved it or not. Being a teacher in a Newark public high school was not a walk in the park. I recall my first day in wood shop. I saw a Puerto Rican boy sanding a piece of wood that was held in a vice. I asked him what he was making.

He said, "A zip gun."

A zip gun is a crude weapon that can fire a bullet with a nail and an elastic band. When the teacher walked into the class, I warned the kid that the teacher had walked in, but he kept working.

The teacher walked up to the kid, took the wood out of the vice, ran his hand over the wood and said, "It needs more sanding."

Despite all these troublesome students, with their varied personalities and backgrounds, the school functioned very well. If you wanted to learn, you could do so.

The first two years at East Side High School were uneventful, but when summer vacation came, I managed to get a part time job at the J&B Cookie Company on Mulberry Street in downtown Newark. I worked for four to six hours every Saturday. The pay was a dollar an hour—even back then it was not a lot of money. The name J&B Cookie Company is very misleading. The "company" was nothing more than a store selling cookies. There were racks on the walls of the store that were mounted at a slight upward angle that held the boxes of cookies in place. We used box cutters to remove the lid of the box, then replace it with an aluminum frame, which had two sliding Plexiglas doors. Once mounted, you could slide the doors open to retrieve the cookies. When someone wanted to buy a particular cookie, we would open the door on the box, reach in, and place the cookies in a brown paper bag, with the customer usually watching. We sold by the pound, and there was a scale located in the middle of the wall so we could weigh the bags. Besides selling cookies, we also sold candy, Italian bread, and small wrapped cakes, the type someone would give her kid for school.

The owner of the store was Jacob (Jake) Boxer. He was a short man, about five-foot-three, and he had an enormous nose. At the time that I worked there, he must have been in his late eighties. I also should mention that Mr. Boxer was a multi-millionaire. Why he bothered with this store was beyond me. As an incentive for working in the store, Jake would give the workers a dollar for lunch. Usually, there were two of us guys working with Jake on Saturdays, because Saturday was the busiest day for the store. On the first day I worked there, the other guy, named Robbie, warned me to never buy a Coca-Cola. If Jake saw you drinking a Coke, Robbie said, he would hit the roof and possibly fire you. The reason was simple: Jake owned thousands of shares in *Pepsi-Cola* and if he saw his employees drinking *Coca-Cola*, he felt they were taking money out of his pocket.

When the store got busy, we worked very hard assisting the customers. This was especially true when the people got their welfare checks. With two workers and Jake filling bags of cookies, it did not take long for the floor to be covered with crushed cookies. On my first day, seeing the mess on the floor, I went into the back room and got a broom and dust pan and swept the floor. Jake was out of the store at the time, but when he returned, it was just in time to see me empty the dust pan into the garbage.

Jake started to scream, "*What are you doing?*" He grabbed my sleeve and pulled me to the center of the store. He pointed to a cardboard box that was under the shelf with the scale. On the box, written in a blue marking pen, were the words, "BROKEN COOKIE MIX! 10 CENTS A POUND." I looked into the box and saw not only broken cookies, but also cigarette butts, used matches, pieces of paper and dirt. Although he insisted that I follow his policy of selling his dirt, I never did. I swept the floor when Jake was not around, and whatever I picked up in the pan was deposited into the garbage. Almost all of the customers were poor and, on occasion, at ten cents a pound, we would have a buyer. I steered the people away from it. Jake, rather than lose a sale, would guide people to it.

When it came to selling candy, Jake had a fool-proof way to turn a profit. He attached a string under the tray of the scale, and the other end of the string had a piece of cardboard attached to it, half floating near the floor. With his foot pressing down on the cardboard, he could add a quarter of a pound to the weight on the scale. When he started putting candy on the scale, he would press down on the cardboard, so if a customer wanted a half pound of chocolate, he got only a quarter pound, thanks to Jake's gadget.

The little cakes we sold were the product of the Jane Parker bakery in Newark. Jane Parker was the brand name for the A&P supermarkets. When the unsold cakes were returned to the bakery by the supermarkets, they were placed in fifty-gallon cardboard drums for disposal. Jake would drive his Chevrolet Impala to the loading dock of the bakery and slip the janitor five dollars for a drum of these returned cakes. Jake told the janitor that he was a pig farmer, and the pigs liked these cakes. After his car was loaded, Jake would drive to the store and tell us to unload the supplies. Once inside the store, Jake would line the top of the counter with rows of these cakes. Sometimes mixed in with these little cakes would be a large pound cake, with or without icing. If Jake saw a bit of green mold on the cake, he would jab his finger through the wrapper and push the mold into the center of the cake. On one particular day, I took out a pound cake where the lemon icing had turned green from mold. I showed Jake and wanted to know what to do with it. He pulled out his marker and made a sign that read, "St. Patty's Day Cake! $1.00" and placed it back on the counter.

It was not uncommon for a young boy or girl to come into the store begging for any kind of food. If Jake was not around, we would gave them either some cookies or a few Italian rolls, and always warned them not to say anything about getting the food from us. One day, a young girl came into the store with her younger brother. She must have been six or seven years old and her brother about three. They walked up to Jake and asked him for something to eat. Jake grabbed the girl and the boy by their arms and threw them onto the sidewalk. It was a terrible thing to witness, and to this day I can still remember the girl and boy crying in front of the store. To Jake, charity was a weakness, and he said he hadn't made his fortune by being generous to the poor.

Just when I thought I had seen it all, I learned about Jake's "refrigerator." My brother was working behind the counter one day when a man stopped in and bought a half dozen Italian rolls. He told my brother that Jake always put his bread in the refrigerator, so that when he came home from work, the bread would still be fresh. My brother took the bag and walked to the back of the storeroom, looking for a refrigerator. A few moments later, he came back into the store where Jake was talking to the man. My brother said, "We don't *have* a refrigerator!" Jake turned to the man and said, "Kids today are so stupid they don't know what a refrigerator looks like!" He grabbed the bag from my brother's hand and walked out of the store, into the storeroom and into the bathroom, placing the bag on the toilet tank. "*This* is what a refrigerator looks like!" he told my brother.

Jake made the Christmas season very special. On one of the top shelves in the store were round tin boxes in which holiday hard candy was sold. These tins dated back to the 1950s and were decorated with images of seasonal paintings from the Currier and Ives collection. If you took a close look at those tins, you would see screwdriver marks around the edges, letting you know that the tins were not new. Early one day, Jake asked me to bring those tins down from the shelf, then to follow him down to the basement. He grabbed a hammer and headed for the basement door.

As we started to walk down the stairs, he took the hammer and pounded the walls. I asked him why he was doing that. He said, "It chases the rats away." Once in the basement, I saw a huge box that had the Christmas hard candy in it. Through the dust, I could read the date markings, which made the candy over ten years old. The rats had been burrowing into the box from the side, but that did not deter Jake. Because of the summer heat, the candy was a solid mass. With the hammer, Jake slammed the sides of the box, loosening up the candy. Soon, I was able to bring up shopping bags of the candy. Jake made two pound bags of the candy and placed it in each tin.

Every Christmas when someone wanted to buy a tin of candy, Jake would say, "Brother, I want to save you money. If I sell you the candy *with* the tin box, I'll have to charge you twice the amount, just because of that tin box. I'll tell you what I'll do, brother. I'll take the candy out, and you can have it for just the cost of the candy." This logic worked for years. Knowing that his customer base was made up of poor people, he used this trick to sell Christmas candy. Those Christmas tins were the most important factor in his whole scheme.

One day, a well-dressed black man came into the store. He walked up to the counter and wanted to buy Christmas candy in the tin box. I explained to him the "deal" he could have, to buy the candy cheaper by not buying the tin, but he would not have it. He wanted the candy in the tin box, period. Jake came up next to me and pushed me out of the way and repeated to the man his cheaper candy deal, but the man wanted no part of it. *He wanted the candy in the tin!* Words between Jake and the man started to get heated, but the man stuck to his plan, and Jake had to sell him the candy with the tin. As soon as the door shut behind the man, Jake took his pen out of his pocket and threw it at the door yelling, "You stupid *idiot!*" and a lot of cruel racial slurs. I bet this kind of marketing is never taught in business schools!

What ever became of Jake Boxer, you might ask? One Saturday, as my brother walked to work, he saw police cars parked in the front of the store. He approached the police at the door and told them that he worked there. "Not today," the policeman told him. Your boss was killed this morning. Looks like someone took a hammer to his head."

Jake the multi-millionaire was gone. My days at working in the cookie store were no more. The man who had exploited these poor people for years was no more. How fitting that he was found lying dead in a pool of blood, just a few feet from his box of ten cents a pound "broken cookie mix."

When summer was over, it was back to school and back to the drudgery of studies. I tried to work hard like everyone else, but I was just an average student. I joined the high school marching band and had a rock and roll group of my own on the side. The rock group, called "Cringe," helped me cope with much of the negativity in my life. It was an artistic release and, through the music, I was able to vent my frustrations through the lyrics. As time passed, the band's music and performances got better and better. We performed for a few college parties, arranged by my brother who was attending St. Peter's College in Jersey City. The college students really liked our music, especially the lyrics. The college newspaper sometimes printed the lyrics to one of our songs. Not bad for a bunch of Newark kids. The band improved, but it was my schooling that needed improving badly. I had to do something and it had to be soon.

In my third year in high school, I finally made a breakthrough. Rather than disregard the strange images and feelings that came to me, I embraced them. That entire summer, I thought about my situation and what I had to do to change it. I began my junior year with a different mindset and a totally different attitude. Whenever possible, I would read each teacher, and I knew what he or she was about to teach. I could sense what was on upcoming tests, and knew the quirks of each teacher. During the first cycle, I put it to the test and just let it happen. My test scores went through the roof. Teachers were amazed at the change in me. When our report cards were handed out, my homeroom teacher, Mr. Corso, glanced at my grades, then took the report card and started walking down the aisle toward my desk with an angry look on his face. I saw him approaching, but paid him no mind. I was seated near the back of the classroom, wearing my blue denim jacket and ankle boots, which I wore every day—it was a type of "uniform" our rock band had adopted.

I was not a troublemaker, so it came as a shock to me when he grabbed my arm and pulled me out of the seat. When I got to my feet, he started pushing me towards the door. I had no idea what this was all about. When we reached the hall, he said, "Did you think you could change the grades on your report card and get away with it?" he asked me as he pushed me into the hall.

The pushing continued right into the principal's office. The vice-principal came out and asked what the problem was. Mr. Corso told him that I had changed the grades on my report card.

"He's a C student and he's changed them to all A's!"

"Wait right here," the vice-principal said as he walked into his office.

He came out a few minutes later and said, "He really got the A's. He's on the Superior Honor's list."

Mr. Corso apologized to me, and we went back to homeroom. I did not get angry with him, though. I understood his surprise. Yet, this whole incident was the proof I had been waiting for.

There was a class I took called "Distributive Education," which was part of a national organization called DECA (Distributive Education Clubs of America). The premise of the course dealt with marketing and sales of products and services. I used the textbook as a reference, but I used my abilities to excel in the class. A few months into the year, the teacher, Mr. "G.," said to me that an 'A' was the highest grade I could get, but I deserved more, so he made me an assistant teacher. On various occasions, Mr. G. asked me to teach the class while he ran an errand or went for a smoke in the teachers' lounge.

Later that year, I entered and won a citywide contest held by DECA and was selected to represent the city of Newark in a statewide competition held in Atlantic City. I was working for a trucking company after school, and I wrote an extensive report on the consolidation, sorting, distribution, and delivery of goods by the trucking industry. Not only was this conference a first for me, but also for the city and our school. Mr. G. and I rode down to Atlantic City in his car; it was the first time I had ever visited Atlantic City.

Once we arrived at the hotel conference center, Mr. G. submitted my entry to the judges. As the entries were being reviewed, a judge motioned to my teacher to come up to his table. The judge told my teacher to prepare me to accept the winning award. Mr. G. came back to the table all smiles, and then we went over how I was to accept this award, step by step.

At our table, we sat with representatives from four schools from different parts of the state. One of the teachers decided that we should introduce ourselves, so each one of us gave his name and the school he was representing.

"Karl Petry, from East Side High School, in Newark," I proudly stated.

Everyone seated at the table glanced at one another as if a leper was amongst them and within a matter of minutes, Mr. G. and I were sitting at the table alone. Mr. G. turned to me and said, "I'm sorry," but the worst was yet to come. As they called out the names of the winners, we discovered I was not one of them. Mr. G. became angry. When the room cleared, he went up to the judges and asked them why I had not won. One judge said that they could not give the award to someone from Newark. Then, after seeing Mr. G.'s red face ready to explode, he quickly added, "Because this was the first year Newark made a submission. It wouldn't look right."

They would never get away with that today, but they could back then. This act of prejudice was no stranger to me. Living in Newark had a stigma attached to it that all of us who lived there knew well. I showed no anger or disappointment, and I did not complain. I just sat back and enjoyed my first trip to Atlantic City. This ability of mine had brought up my grade point average, gotten my parents off my back for failing grades and, in this case, had won me a one-day mini-vacation to the Jersey shore.

Those last two years of high school were the easiest I'd ever had, but I still did not know the full extent of my ability, or what it was, or even how to describe it. There was no discussing this with others: I was afraid to look foolish. I was just seventeen, and looking foolish is a fate worse than death for every seventeen-year-old boy or girl in the world.

One interesting development happened in my last year of high school. At the start of my senior year, I was seated in the band room in the saxophone section. I played alto sax, and Brian Speck, who was sitting to my right, played tenor. It was the first day of school and the first time we were seeing the new band members. I don't know how it is in other schools, but it seemed like every kid who signed up to be in the marching band in our school wanted to be a drummer. At least ten guys came in with that in mind. The teacher quickly sorted out the drummer overflow, keeping a few and sending the rest back to the guidance counselor's office.

In the flute section was a cute, small, dark-haired girl. The teacher started the roll call and called out, "Sueli DeCarvalho." That cute girl said, "Here."

I looked at Brian and said, "I'm going to marry that girl." He just smirked, but true to my word, within a few years, *I married that girl!*

In this chapter you witnessed the first seventeen years of my life, starting from infancy to being a very confused teenager. Past generations have often overlooked these teenage years. Adults just mark it off as "the awkward years" of youth, a time a person just has to endure until he or she comes to their senses and enters adulthood. To make a stand about the existence of psychic phenomena at this time in my life would have made me a target of laughter, pity, and hate. As a teenager, I was wise to keep quiet about all this.

A milestone in an effort to change the way people perceived the lives of teenagers came in 1955 when the film *Rebel Without A Cause* was released. Finally, a major film brought home that fact that teenagers are real people and have feelings that should be taken seriously. The film's star, James Dean, portrayed a teenage character named Jim Stark, whose awkwardness, sensitivity, love, and caring highlighted the danger of being "different" from his peers. The lesson of danger certainly hit home with me.

Should I have insisted that the visions I experienced were real, it would have surely alienated me from my peers and teachers, as well as from my entire family. My life would have been unbearable, and worse, I could have been tagged as a person with a serious mental problem. Those teenage years would keep me tight lipped for many years, but despite how hard I tried to hide my psychic ability, its effect would always surface from time to time. A person can suppress psychic ability. I could bottle it up, but there was no guarantee that I could always keep a lid on it.

From time to time I found it personally entertaining to show off my ability to others, almost like doing a few magic tricks for your friends. When I had the ear of someone who expressed an interest in the paranormal, I would open up a side of me they never knew or expected. I was good at selecting those to whom I could talk about all this.

I met a school teacher, Alice, who taught at Parsippany High School. I would, on occasion, speak to schools about interesting stories mostly unknown in American history. To enhance my presentations, I brought props that I had collected over the years, like army helmets and rare tin photographs. Alice told me about her belief in the paranormal, which led me to disclose my abilities to her and later to her family. After my visit to the school, we met at her house, where she introduced me to her daughter and son.

I began by looking at the mother and describing the images I saw from her past. I saw her in the 1950s entering a candy store and buying an ice cream cone, then leaving the store while eating the cone, then turning the corner and seeing her school. She was amazed at the accuracy of the details I described. She told me this had been a normal event in her day-to-day life when she attended high school. She loved ice cream—it was her childhood addiction. We all laughed about it. My demonstration was an amusing diversion.

When it was time for me to leave, I made my way through the kitchen, and noticed on the wall a board with a display of tiny spoons, the type used to feed babies. I placed my hand on each spoon, moving from row to row, then I stopped at one particular spoon and said, "This spoon was not used for a baby. It was used by an older woman for her tea."

The reaction from the family was suddenly solemn. I thought, "Congratulations, Karl. You did it again. You took a nice, entertaining visit and made it into a serious paranormal event." It turned out that the spoon had once belonged to Alice's aunt, who used it only for stirring her tea. She never had children and died a sad and lonely woman. Alice asked if I could tell her what her aunt looked like. "She has on a blue dress, has hair down to her shoulders, and it's gray with streaks of black in it." Once again, I was accurate, but accuracy was a high price to pay for ruining the mood of the day.

In the weeks that followed, I became good friends with the family and opened up about how my psychic ability was not all fun, and that it was a burden in my life. I explained about the visions that constantly popped up wherever I went. I described the sleepless nights, sometimes lasting for many nights, and, that when I met people for the first time, I would see images of their lives hovering like a small television over their right shoulders. Simply put, it was too much input for any person to handle. I was often on sensory overload, I told them, and this overload made for a depressing existence.

Taking my words to heart, Alice wanted to help. She discovered that a Catholic priest in the Central New Jersey town of Summit had started a program to help people with psychic abilities. His group would discuss psychic phenomena and how to cope with this gift. Heading this program was Father Morris. For me, looking to the Catholic Church for help with my problem went against the grain. After the years I spent in St. Casimir's School, enduring the sisters' mental and physical brutality toward the students, the idea of enlisting the help of a Catholic priest seemed out of the question. I voiced my concern to Alice, but she assured me that he was different and it was worth the trip to see him.

"Father Morris also has psychic abilities and understands the problems attached to it," she said.

With nothing to lose, I phoned Father Morris and briefly told him of my situation. He said that his group would be meeting Saturday at the church's rectory, and he invited me to meet with him at three in the afternoon.

I arrived early at the church that Saturday. The church was enormous and looked more like a cathedral than your typical neighborhood parish church. The rectory next to the church was similarly built and stood two stories high. Since I was early, I took a walk to the center of town just a block away and checked out the local stores. I had time to have a cup of coffee at a cafe just around the corner from the church. Seated at the window, I was sipping my coffee watching as the locals went about their shopping. From the clothing the people wore and the cars they drove, it was apparent that this was a wealthy town, compared to Kearny where I was living. I wondered what these people would think if they knew that the only reason I came to Summit was to discuss my psychic ability with their parish priest, who also claimed to be psychic.

It was almost three, so I left the cafe and went to the rectory. No one could be seen on the lawns surrounding the property. I pushed open the large doors to the building and found myself alone. The interior had large, dark wood moldings, giving me the impression of a gothic castle. Then I heard the sound of young people laughing on the second floor and what seemed like running across the floor. I started walking up the stairway to the second floor where the noise got louder. At the top of the stairs, I could see at the end of the floor a priest seated in a small office facing the open floor and stairway. I slowly walked toward the priest, who stared at me as I approached him. Getting closer, the look on the priest's face gave me the impression that he was afraid.

Before I could say a word, the priest said, "You're Karl Petry."

"How did you know?" I asked.

"I sensed it the minute you walked into the building." He pointed to the seat in front of his desk and asked me to have a seat. I related to him the problems I was having and my ability to see rooms and buildings change to a previous time right in front of me. He gave me a confused look as if he did not understand what I was saying.

To clarify my point, I said, "There was once a window behind you that has been bricked up and there was a chair molding that was around this room that has been removed."

Father Morris sat quietly for about twenty seconds, then said, "The window was removed about eight years ago, along with the molding."

I did not say a word. Frankly, I didn't know what to say. With his elbows resting on the arms of the chair, he formed a point with his fingers that touched the bridge of his nose. Suddenly he dropped his arms and said, "You're beyond anything we have here."

He talked about his program that seemed to be focused more on children. There were about ten young boys and girls on the floor and he made sure he did not single out any one of the children that happened to be there. Father Morris then suggested that I contact the Parapsychology Foundation in New York City.

The trip confirmed that I was on the right track and that I was no longer facing this psychic thing alone. I learned there are people who believe in this force and who would listen to me and not be judgmental. This would not be an easy road to take, because most people *are* judgmental and will take any opportunity to ridicule someone who is "different." I also learned that, although my Catholic past had been at times brutal, I had to find it within myself not to dismiss everyone connected to the Catholic Church. I was now thirty-nine years old and it seemed that I was officially accepted as a psychic—and that confirmation had come from, of all things, a Catholic priest.

I decided to venture to the Parapsychology Foundation on Monday, April 27, 1992. It was a bright, sunny day in the low 60s when I boarded the PATH train in Harrison, New Jersey. I got off at the 33rd Street platform, which is under Macy's department store. Once there, I took a taxi the rest of the way to 228 East 71st Street. I stood in front of the building for a moment before I walked in.

Once past the door, I noticed this was a library—the Eileen Garrett Library to be exact, according to the plaque that was mounted on the building. I was not quite sure what to expect from the people here, or how I was to be perceived the minute I opened my mouth about being a psychic. I was very anxious about this next step I was about to take, but I kept in the back of my mind that this place had been recommended by Father Morris, so how bad could it be?

No one approached me as I walked in. Seated at a desk in the middle of the room was an attractive woman with blonde hair in a smart-looking business suit. I introduced myself and told her that Father Morris of Summit had recommended that I visit this place.

The woman was Dr. Joanne D.S. McMahon. She was the director of the Eileen J. Garrett Library and the "go to" person if you had questions. I explained the strange experiences I was having and the problems connected to them. With each claim I made, Dr. McMahon remained calm and did not flinch a bit. In fact, she had an explanation for each of my abilities and told me that what I was experiencing were well-known phenomena in parapsychology. She took it all in stride, as if my stopping in to talk about such things was a daily occurrence for her. This was the start of a beautiful friendship.

Joanne D.S. McMahon

Finally, after all this time, I had someone who could answer intelligently the questions I had about not only my psychic ability but the field of parapsychology in general. For so many years I had been hiding within myself. I had wanted to share what I was seeing and experiencing with others, but I had always played it safe. I had restrained my urges and kept quiet. Now I had a colleague and a friend with whom I could share everything that had happened to me. I was no longer alone.

I had already made a rule for myself, which I still hold to this day: I will not read any books written by psychics. Psychics usually tell the reader about their experiences and give explanations about how their powers work. Reading these books tends to confuse me, because my experiences of how I see things are often different from theirs. I would often wonder, while reading a book by another psychic, "Am I doing something wrong?" Dr. McMahon understood my concern and agreed to my self-imposed ban on reading other psychics' books.

Over the coming weeks and months, Dr. McMahon was kind enough to take my many phone calls and answer what seemed to be hundreds of questions, helping me to make sense of my psychic ability. I guess when she was satisfied that I was not a raving lunatic, she invited me to her home. Joanne and her husband, Tom, were wonderful hosts and, after a tour of their home, we all settled in the living room for some friendly chitchatting over a few glasses of wine.

Joanne asked, "What prompted you to come forward and openly talk to people about your psychic ability?"

I sat quietly for a few moments, bringing that memory to the forefront of my mind, while Tom refilled our glasses. I decided to tell my story. Rather than just tell her about what sparked my "coming out" to the public about my situation, I wanted her to know something about my life—those early years leading up to this moment. This is the story I told her.

The "coming out" happened one day as I was sitting at a Dunkin Donuts on Washington Avenue in Nutley, New Jersey. On this day at this place, I experienced my epiphany. As I sat looking out of the window, sipping my coffee, the noise in the store began to fade away. Suddenly, it was completely silent. Looking back at the serving counter, I observed the people in line and the two female servers moving in slow motion and in complete silence. I turned quickly toward the window and saw Washington Avenue, but as it looked in the late 1920s or early 1930s. I was startled by the scene of two Model A cars passing each other on this cobblestone street and the countless number of wires suspended from poles, running in all directions. My mind took in all this information, yet the entire experience lasted for about five seconds. I had witnessed a clip of time, years before I was born, a time snatched from the past, with no known reason or explanation behind this vision.

As fast as this all happened, it ended. The ambient noise in the doughnut emporium returned as I heard a crackling voice say, "Two glazed, two sugar, and two old fashioned," which rang out from the server in front of the doughnut rack.

This sort of experience had happened to me numerous times before, but this time I wanted to share my vision. A man whose age I guessed as late seventies was sitting next to me, facing the street, as I was during this entire episode. He seemed preoccupied and unaware of my presence and certainly had no way of knowing what I had just been through.

I turned to him and said, "This place has certainly changed over the years, hasn't it?"

I proceeded to describe the building across the street as it once looked. I "reminisced" about the trolley tracks and the massive number of wires running from pole to pole. After taking the last bite of his doughnut, he just grinned and confirmed what I had said.

"Back then, if they put up any more wires on those poles, they'd have blocked out the sun!" he laughingly said. He never even questioned where I had obtained that information, probably thinking I must have been told about this from someone *his* age, because I was much too young to have seen it firsthand.

My story certainly had the attention of Joanne and Tom. Even their dog, Calvin, seemed to be listening intently. Like Joanne, Tom was also a good listener. I guess over the years, being married to a parapsychologist, he'd heard it all.

In a short time, I went from being a reclusive psychic to someone who could at least talk to select people who were non-judgmental and understood psychic ability. With the help of good friends, Father Morris, and Dr. McMahon of the Parapsychology Foundation, I was well on my way. I had turned an important corner in my life.

Another important person I met at the Parapsychology Foundation was George Hansen, a parapsychologist, author, and researcher. George has helped me a great deal in my career. I've always found him to be interesting, personable and a delightful conversationalist. George won't speculate on a topic; rather, he will wait until he has enough factual and solid information before making his opinion known. You would think someone with a personality like his would be the complete opposite of me, and he is. When he has enough solid information on a subject he will take a stand, and he isn't intimidated by who is there to challenge him.

George Hansen

I once heard a respected professor from the University of Maryland call George a "fuck'n bulldog." Here is a fine example of this. George once asked me to videotape a talk he was giving at the Community College of Philadelphia. The subject was supposed to be, "The Psychic, The Paranormal and the Supernatural." However, after hearing a few minutes of his talk, I thought it should have been called, "Attack On Skeptics." His attack was so powerful that during the taping I hoped there were no skeptics in the audience. Glancing down at the program announcement next to me, I realized that this audience *was* a skeptic group! The only thing I had to wait for was the fistfight I expected before his talk was over. It never happened, which goes to show you, miracles do happen.

From time to time I refer to George's book, *The Trickster and the Paranormal*, to get an insight into various subjects dealing with the paranormal. Whenever I have a question about something that comes up in my cases, I just make a call to George, and he always has an answer.

Since those early days, my career as a psychic has unfolded in ways I never would have imagined. I have been guided, perhaps by unseen spiritual powers, to talk to the dead and the dying, to help souls cross over, and to help the living come to terms with the great gulf of death. The path has not been easy, and it is often lonely, but I walk it with confidence, knowing that I bring a much needed light to the darkness.

4

Entering the Mind of the Dying

At 7:30 PM on a cold December evening, I hopped into my GMC Jimmy, started the engine and turned up the dial on the radio. The Rolling Stones singing *Get Off Of My Cloud* boomed out. As I headed my truck down the street, I turned the volume up a tad to block all the ambient noise outside. I needed the distraction to clear my head and concentrate on my trip to the Clara Maass Medical Center in Belleville, New Jersey. People were waiting for me in the intensive care unit: Christine, the wife of a friend of mine, and her daughter, Linda. Both had spent hours that day at the bedside of Christine's mother, Maria, who was in a coma and on life support—and not expected to live much longer. Christine and Linda had to make a decision, and they were asking me for help.

I made my right turn off Franklin Avenue and onto the hospital entrance road. It was a cold night, so back into the closet had gone my lightweight jacket. I had decided to wear my thick, black coat. I was prepared to walk the entire length of the parking lot, as I am usually not lucky enough to find a spot close to the building.

As I drove up the winding hospital access road, I was surprised that, given the size of the hospital, there was not a single person walking the grounds. The stillness of the night, the absence of people, and the parking lot lights that cast a purple tint on the cars and walkways, combined to create an eerie look.

I parked my truck at the end of the second parking lot and headed for the reception area. Once inside the building, I was greeted by an empty desk, so I walked to the hospital directory hanging on the wall to find the location of the intensive care unit. Upon entering the elevator, I glanced at my watch. It was 8 PM. As I exited the elevator and stepped onto the floor, the only sound I could hear was the hissing of respirators clicking on and off. This was the sound of fragile lives hanging in the balance.

A doctor and an orderly turned quickly around to look at me as I entered the ward through the metal swinging doors. Since I was dressed totally in black, they probably thought I was a priest, called to perform the last rights for a dying patient.

Halfway into a room on the right, I caught sight of Christine and Linda next to the bed where Maria lay. Christine and Linda looked exhausted from the hours they had been spending there. Only a few words were exchanged between us. There was no need for conversation, because we all knew why I was there.

Earlier that afternoon at the hospital, Christine and her brother, Paul, were told by the doctor treating their mother that there was no sign of brain activity, and he suggested that they should remove Maria from life support. Christine had refused, because she wanted proof that her mother was truly gone. That was when I got the call to come to the hospital. Christine was leaving it up to me to determine if Maria's mind was still active, or if she was "totally gone" as the doctors claimed.

I removed my coat while Linda pulled up a chair for me next to the bed. I sat down and explained to them what I was about to do. This procedure was nothing new to me. I had done this many times.

"I will bring my presence into the mind of Maria," I said. "I will enter Maria's dream state, introduce myself, and try to get her to accept me as a friend or a messenger, allowing me to relay any words or mental images from her to members of her family. If I try to reach her and there is nothing but a blank void, I will tell you." A blank void, I explained, would indicate that there was no brain activity. Then the family could decide about releasing Maria from life support.

Linda stood next to the dividing curtain drawn around Maria's bed while Christine sat in one of the light-colored, wooden arm chairs. They watched as I positioned myself next to the bed. I briefly looked up to see, at the far corner of the room, a nurse watching my every move.

I began by taking my left hand and touching the right side of Maria's face. With deep concentration, I began my journey into her mind. In the past, with other comatose patients, this had taken just a few moments, but Maria proved to be harder to reach. Minutes passed, and I was still getting nothing. There was little doubt in my mind that this woman still had brain activity, but she would not let me in.

I looked up at Christine and said, "She's being stubborn and won't let me in."

More time went by and *still* Maria would not allow me access. I turned to Christine and asked, "Is your mother a stubborn woman?"

Christine laughed and said, "You bet!"

Finally, after about twenty-five minutes, Maria let me in. I began to hear voices speaking in Italian. I cannot speak or understand Italian. *Now what?* I wondered.

I asked Christine, "Does your mother speak Italian?"

"Well, maybe just a little," Christine answered. I repeated the words I had heard, in my heavy, American-accented Italian. Linda got out a tablet and used a translation program to translate what I was saying. Apparently I was calling out the names of towns in Italy. The information caused images to flow through my mind of women sitting on benches in front of closely-built row houses. Then it all started to make sense.

"Is your mother from the North Ward of Newark?" I asked.

"Yes," Christine answered.

Now I understood what Maria was mentally showing me: where she had grown up. The North Ward of Newark was the Italian section of the city, and the women I was seeing and hearing were discussing their hometowns in Italy. My guess of the time period was mid- to late 1920s. New Jersey summers can be quite brutal, especially in a large, concrete-covered city like Newark. In those days, there were no air conditioners. You would be lucky just to have a fan in your apartment. Back then, it was a common practice for the women to take benches stored in the alleys between the houses and drag them to the front of the house facing the street. Gossip would run wild and talks of "the old country" were commonplace.

Those images flowed through me at an incredible speed. In a flash, Maria took me to the neighborhood streets of her youth. Then, like a flash of lighting, she fast-forwarded me to a more recent Italian street festival. The images of that festival were so strong that I felt as if I were standing next to her at the feast. I realized that she was a heavy smoker. Many of my images of the festival were through clouds of Maria's cigarette smoke. In a strong voice, she called out to a man named "Romeo" and asked if he wanted a slice of pie (real Italians always referred to pizza as "pie.") Then I heard ringing in my ears, and the sounds and images of the festival started to fade.

I knew Maria was getting tired, and it was time for me to leave her world and return to mine. I woke from my self-imposed trance and asked Christine if she knew someone named Romeo. She did not. I paused, and then delivered the news I had been called to deliver.

"Your mother still has an active mind and she is now reliving her life in dreams," I said.

My visit put the life-or-death decision on hold. As far as the family was concerned, there would be no disconnecting any tubes or wires—not until she was truly gone.

The next day, Maria's family took a morning break from the hospital vigil and gathered at Christine's house to rest and eat before returning to the hospital. I joined them, and there I met Christine's sister-in-law, Joan. My talk of Maria's trip to the Italian feast the night before stirred up some fond family memories, and during breakfast, Christine mentioned to Joan about all the Italian festivals they had gone to as kids. Joan recalled going with Christine's mother to the last one a few months back, joined by Maria's new neighbor, "Romeo." I did not say a word. I did not have to. With just that one comment, Christine and Linda were truly convinced that Maria's brain was still active, and I was accurately delivering her thoughts to the family.

A few days passed, and then it was time for me to visit Maria again. I made plans and called Christine to tell her to expect me the next day.

That night, however, an image of Maria came to me as I slept. She was wearing a yellow kerchief around her head. She had a slight smile and was showing me a square box. She opened the box and pulled out a crucifix. It was made out of wood and was about six inches long.

The next morning, Gary, Christine's husband, called to tell me Christine's mother had died during the previous night. I withheld the information I had received while in my dream state until I met Gary in person the next day. I told Gary, who, in turn told Christine, about Maria's visitation to me and the box and crucifix her mother had shown me. But follow-up would have to wait, for there were a funeral and burial to plan and attend, and the daunting job of clearing out Maria's apartment.

Many guests came to the wake. Maria and her family had many friends, including quite a few members of Gary's Freemason lodge. I knew only the immediate family and the lodge members who stopped by, so I sat in the back of the funeral parlor and watched the people filing past the casket and offering their condolences to the family. A curious thought went through my head: I was the last person Maria spoke to in life, and here I was, quietly tucked away in the last row of the viewing room.

The day of the burial came and went as if it were a dream. During mourning, there doesn't seem to be anything a person can say to the bereaved that will make the pain of loss easier to bear. The daily affairs of life have to carry on. A landlord can be sympathetic, but by the end of the month, he wants that apartment empty.

Paul got his hands on a truck, and along with Gary and his son, Joey, Paul's son, David, and I, we all met at the apartment early on Saturday. We removed the furniture from the apartment and trucked it over to a storage facility a few miles away in Bloomfield. With the larger items gone, it was up to Christine and her brother, Paul, to gather up all the small items and empty the apartment completely.

Paul was not open to the belief in the paranormal. He was an accountant, and it was his nature to believe only in tangibles, like what you would put on a line on a ledger sheet. He had been told about my dream visit from Maria. His skepticism lost ground as he picked up a yellow kerchief in the closet, exactly as I had described it to the family from my dream. Paul was visibly shaken by the discovery of this yellow kerchief.

As the cleaning continued, Christine came across crucifixes her mother had stashed throughout the rooms over the years. When she found one, she would phone me and describe it, hoping she had found the one I had seen in my dream. Every call resulted in the same reply from me: "No, that's not it."

Christine went to the apartment every day to sort through both the wanted and unwanted items. By the end of the week, the apartment was in its final stage of cleaning. Not much was left, and there was still no sign of the elusive cross. The end of the month was drawing near, and there were only a few days left before Maria's apartment had to be vacated.

On one of the last days, Christine was leaving the apartment when a feeling came over her and caused her to go back into one of the rooms. She walked to the closet just off the kitchen that still had towels neatly stacked in it, and almost, as if by command, she reached into the center of the stack of towels and pulled out a box.

It was a square box, just as I had described it from my vision. She opened the box and found the crucifix Maria had shown to me, along with photos and baby items of her first child, who had died in 1946. The baby's name had been Anthony. The crucifix had been displayed in Anthony's casket during the viewing, and just before the burial. Maria had removed it and placed it in this small box with other mementoes, including a pair of baby shoes and Anthony's prayer card. Apparently, Maria, through her final vision to me, wanted her daughter and son to find and keep this box full of her cherished memories, and not to have it carelessly discarded in a rush to clean the apartment. I am sure Maria felt as I do, that in life these are the things that are the most precious.

This story does not end with the burial, nor does it end with the finding of the box. I wish it did. I would be involved with these same people once again in a similar situation. It all seems ironic, just like a case of lightning striking twice in the same place.

Six months later, Paul was diagnosed with terminal lung cancer. In his final days, Christine spent many hours with him at the hospital, just as she had a year before with her mother. When they were alone, Paul told Christine that their Mom's spirit was visiting him in the hospital. This was no surprise to Christine, because the relationship between Paul and his mother had been very strong. Christine asked Paul if, when he crossed over, he could somehow let her know that he was okay. Paul replied that he would try to do it, if not through her, then through me. The evidence of the yellow kerchief seemed to have finally convinced Paul that the psychic phenomena I had experienced the previous year was real.

My nights were filled with emotional and mental stress due to Paul's failing condition. During the day, I could mentally see him in his hospital bed. I felt the end was near, and there was nothing I could do to help him, except to wait patiently for the end. One night, as I was tossing and turning, the image of Paul came into my mind, but this time it was different. Paul was younger and he had hair, something he had lost many years earlier. In my image, he had a football and was tossing it from one hand to the other. He wore a huge smile on his face and was wearing a New York Jets poncho. This was Paul as I had never known him. Once I understood who I was looking at, he immediately widened his grin, turned, and ran away.

The next morning, Gary called to tell me that Paul had died during the night. It was almost to the day of Maria's death a year earlier. Paul had crossed over and joined his mother.

True to his word to Christine, Paul had visited me on his way out and told me that he was all right. I related the story of his visit to Christine. She said that football was his passion. He had played it in high school and college and was a season ticket holder for the New York Jets. Now, in death, Paul was playing his favorite game and having a great time doing it.

Maria and Paul were gone. What I shared with them in their passing helped to bring closure to Christine and her family, and answered the many questions that people like them have during these times of transition from one life to another.

I was grateful that Paul was able to be open-minded when he saw the evidence of the yellow kerchief. I believe it enabled him to communicate with me in his own transition.

Psychics like me will always be on the outside of mainstream society. Sometimes we are respected for what we do and sometimes we are ridiculed. Over the years, I have found those who profess to be "open-minded" do the most rejecting and criticizing of psychics, and are very vocal about it. Any subject dealing with the paranormal is considered fair game for their wrath. I believe that psychic ability and paranormal phenomena frighten them. To quote Norman Cousins, the famous American political journalist, "*Where man can find no answer, he will find fear.*"

5

Post Mortems

Sometimes my ability to tune in to the dying and the deceased leads to awkward social situations. When I attend funerals and wakes, I often spontaneously pick up on the parting comments of the newly departed. Yes, the dead often attend their final ceremonies. Many people think that death automatically transforms personalities into something angelic, but that is not always the case. What I hear ranges from last loving thoughts to all-too-earthly grumblings.

When I attend the final events, it is not uncommon for all the visitors in the room to stop talking and stare as I enter the viewing room, as if they expect me to put on a show for them. I usually walk from the casket to the immediate family of the deceased to offer my condolences, and then move to an area in the room where I can either mingle with relatives and friends of the family or just sit inconspicuously. On occasion, the people in the room will ask me if the deceased has communicated with me. This puts me in a tough spot. The members of the grieving family would probably be very upset if they overheard paranormal talk concerning their dead family member. When this happens, I usually find a diplomatic way to change the subject or politely walk away.

On a few occasions, I have come across grieving families that encourage what I do, because they themselves are just as curious to find out if their deceased loved one has something to say. People are often surprised to hear that when the dead communicate with me, their personalities are the same in death as they were in life. There are no whispery voices speaking of love and forgiveness and showering the living with messages of hope and peace. To illustrate my point, I'll share with you a few examples of my experiences.

I was at a funeral parlor at the Jersey shore where the father of a good friend of mine was being viewed. The man in life never hesitated to let you know what was on his mind. He was a kind and giving man, but everyone knew that they should never, never try to cheat him or cross him, especially in business. Amongst all the people that knew him, he stood out as a very popular and unique character, and when he died it was a terrible blow to everyone who knew him. His illness lasted a few years, which took its toll on him. The once giant-voiced man lost his voice, and a much smaller and fragile body replaced the powerful girth of the man he once was.

As Sue and I drove to the wake, there was no doubt in our minds that it would be a full house. As I expected, the viewing room was packed. I was standing next to the wall facing the casket when I heard the voice of the deceased loud and clear. *"There's Nick, that son-of-a-bitch, he owes me six thousand dollars, and he thinks because I'm dead, that he won't have to pay it back! That phony bastard."*

It was hard for me to believe that his loud voice coming through so strongly could only be heard by me.

Then a priest walked up to the front of the casket to offer prayers. He was African and spoke with a heavy accent that was hard to understand. As soon as he began his prayers, the voice of the sleeping giant rang out, *"This is the best they could get? No one can understand the son-of-a-bitch!"*

After the prayers, Sue and I quietly left. In the large crowd, we had blended in and few were even aware we were there. I caught a lucky break.

On another occasion, I used to work as a legal videographer for Gloria, who owned a court reporting service. We worked together for more than twenty years. Gloria was a delightful person on both a personal and business level.

One day, I received a call from her office manager, who told me that Gloria's mother died, and Gloria and her family were making final arrangements. The viewing would take place in a few days at a funeral parlor in Westfield, New Jersey.

On a normal day, it would take about thirty minutes for me to drive to Westfield, but on the day of the viewing, there was a snowstorm. The highways were treacherous, with cars sliding from lane to lane. Travelers on the always-busy Route 22 dropped to a cautious twenty-five miles per hour—in New Jersey that is considered very slow. I knew that many people would not be able to make it because of the weather, so I was determined to do whatever it took to get there.

That evening, with the snow still falling at an incredible rate, I arrived to find just a few people in the room. I was greeted at the door by one of the funeral parlor workers. He took my snow-covered coat and hung it up. My shoes were wet and I tracked water throughout this nice carpeted room. I felt guilty, but that feeling left me when I saw another visitor walk in with boots caked with snow, leaving mini-piles of snow from the door to the casket.

I felt everyone's eyes watching me as I waited to approach the casket. I heard Gloria say to her friends, "He's the one."

I looked into the casket. It was the first time I set eyes on Gloria's mother. Then I heard the voice of the deceased woman: *"I told Gloria not to marry that man. I hate him and I don't know why she married him."*

Gloria walked up and stood next to me. "Is my mother saying anything to you?" she asked.

At first I just gave a slight smile. Then I said, "Your mother just told me she doesn't care for your husband."

Gloria answered, "She hated David." She confirmed everything her deceased mother told me. Evidently her mother's displeasure with her choice in a husband was an old story in their household. I did not detect any shocked reaction to my comment. I wouldn't go into details about her mother's comments; I just let the whole thing go. I sat down with Gloria and her friends, chatted for a while, then left.

As an outsider, seldom do I have any idea what the recently deceased will say or whom they are talking about. As far as Gloria's husband David was concerned, he always treated me well, so the comments made by Gloria's mother seemed to come out of left field. It's never for me to judge—I am just someone to whom those who recently passed can say their last words and thoughts.

I don't want to give the impression that the only people who communicate to me after death are angry and want to get their last revengeful word in before they cross over. Such was not the case with Patricia and Ernie Klein.

Ernie worked in the Conoco refinery and Pat was a court reporter. They always worked hard for the things they had and provided a good home for their children. Although Pat and I worked together for many years, I knew little about their family. Through snippets of conversations we had over time, I knew that Ernie's father was having a rough time of it with his health. When I heard that he died, it came as no surprise. The wake for the father, Ernest C. Klein, Sr., was in Linden, the town where they all grew up.

Linden has always been a blue-collar community where many of the inhabitants worked at the refinery. It had been many years since I had visited there. As I drove into town for the wake, the sight of a billboard on the main street written in Polish brought back memories of the store signs I saw growing up in my Polish neighborhood in Newark.

Pat and Ernie had always been fascinated by my abilities, and told many of the mourners at the wake that there was a good chance that I would be stopping by. The moment I walked in, I sensed that people in the room were watching me. The casket was draped in an American flag and pictures were on display from Ernie's dad's military and private life.

I heard a voice, but this voice was speaking with a German accent. An American veteran of World War II speaking with a German accent caught me completely off guard. This voice began to speak in a normal cadence, then escalated to triple-speed. It was so fast that I could only absorb about twenty percent of what I heard.

Ernie's father told me how proud he was of his son and how much he loved his family. Through mental images, he showed me the house where Ernie grew up, and talked about other family members whose names were not familiar to me.

Pat, Ernie, and a few others walked over to me wondering what was happening. I told them of the words and visuals being shown to me by Ernie's dad, and that I was having difficulty catching all the things he was saying. Ernie said that his father had been unable to speak for over a year and he was a man who loved to talk, so he was catching up with the things he had wanted to say for so long.

During his rapid-fire dialogue, he said Ernie was his only son, so I said to Ernie, "So, you're the only son?"

Ernie looked at me and nodded his head in the affirmative. I told him his father just told me that. So, being the man in the middle, I tried my best to be a human tape recorder, and repeated to the family the words and visions I could remember from my dialogue with Ernie's father. It wasn't long before I became extremely fatigued. This relaying of messages always takes a lot out of me. Shortly after, I knew it was time to leave.

I never met this man while he was alive, and that is a pity. I could tell he was an exceptional man and a person I would have readily liked as a friend. No bitterness or anger, just a very nice guy whose time it was to cross life's barrier. Soon after I left the building, the voice was gone, leaving me with fond memories of a man I never knew.

Interestingly, my deceased family members never communicated with me during their wakes or funerals. A few times they came to me later, but never at the wake.

One such incident happened when my mother-in-law, Catherine, passed away. I had a visual visitation only; no words were spoken. Catherine was born in Brazil, but her parents were from

Yugoslavia. Catherine looked like she could easily fit into my family with her baby blue eyes and fair skin. We always got along, from my early days of dating her daughter to the end of her life.

The story of Catherine was not uncommon in our Ironbound neighborhood. My maternal grandmother left Poland with her sisters to find a better life in America. Sue's mother, Catherine, left her family in Brazil, and, with her husband Aristides and three children, immigrated to the United States in 1962 to do the same. They moved from one terrible apartment to another and decided that since the rents were high and the living standard in those apartments were low, they needed to buy their own house. There were two criteria in the purchase of a house: it had to be a two-family so the rental apartment could help pay the mortgage, and it had to be cheap.

Soon a house came on the market and the price was right. They did not even walk through the entire house before deciding to buy it. It wasn't just a house; a better description would be a disaster of a house. Most women would wait until they had enough money to buy a better house, but Catherine knew this might be the only opportunity they had. It was roach-infested and needed repairs everywhere. To rid the house of the horrid roaches, Aristides, or as his co-workers and friends called him, Harry, repeatedly set off an industrial aerosol bug bomb in the basement. A few hours later, he would take a shovel and load the roaches into the garbage. That's how bad the problem was. The cause of the infestation were the previous homeowners, who ran a short-term rooming house in the basement. When cargo ships docked at Port Newark, crew members would leave the ship to wander the streets of the Ironbound, sampling each bar they passed. When the bars closed, this house offered them a no frills, cheap place to sleep where they could lay down on one of the many hammocks attached to the basement walls.

Harry and Catherine had little money but did have carpentry and masonry skills, and within a short time they made both apartments in the building clean, modern and livable—and, most importantly, roach-free. Catherine was a smart woman and when confronted with a bad situation, she would find a way to get out of it. Catherine had no issues with me. When I told her and Harry that I wanted to marry Sue, they were very happy for us.

Sue and I were the first of their children to get married, followed by her sister, Sonia, a year later. Brother Ed stayed single, but not for long. The years flew by, and grandchildren arrived. Sonia had a son, and then a few years' later had twins, a boy and a girl. Ed got married and, shortly after had a son.

With things in Newark running smoothly, Catherine decided to move from Newark to the nearby town of Kearny into a nicer two family home. They kept the Newark house and rented out their old apartment. Life was getting easier and home construction projects were becoming a thing of the past. Things seemed to be looking up, or were they?

While in Newark, Catherine worked at a pharmaceutical factory that made various medicines and vitamin pills. The company was doing well and the workers were encouraged to work six days a week to meet the demand. The production line work and the long hours took a toll on her, and Catherine began to complain about not feeling well. Soon it was obvious to the family that this work was making her sick. When they moved to Kearny, she quit the pharmaceutical company and went to work at a scale manufacturing company in East Hanover. The job was much easier, but her health continued to get worse.

Ed divorced and re-married, to a woman named Lisa. Soon they had a daughter, Alexis. Lisa was pleasant and was very attractive. She had the look that could stop traffic. On the flip side, Lisa's personality was at times abrasive and controlling. Soon this character flaw would come out at the worst possible time.

By the mid-1990s, Catherine was diagnosed with stomach cancer. She went to a cancer specialist and tried every treatment they had to offer. It was hard for the family to see her struggling with this sickness, because we could not help her fight this disease. We all felt helpless.

Catherine died in 1996. The family and I stayed with her in the hospital at bedside to the very end. With her passing, my good buddy was gone. As close as we were, she did not come to me at the wake.

Anyone who ever goes through this kind of tragedy will tell you how difficult it is. A long list of decisions must be made quickly by the family, including picking a casket, reviewing insurance paperwork, and notifying the other family members of the loss. With all this tragic turmoil going on, Lisa, thinking she was helping the family, made this bad situation worse. In an effort to help, she prematurely contacted a funeral parlor in Newark. She had a key for Catherine's apartment, and while Harry and Sue were busy at the hospital, Lisa entered the apartment to look for the gown Catherine had worn to Lisa and Ed's wedding a few years earlier, which the family had agreed would be the burial dress. Not knowing Lisa's plans already in motion, Sue and her father were making arrangements with another funeral parlor, this one in Kearny. In a few hours, Sue got a panicked call from the Kearny funeral parlor, telling her that when they went to the hospital to pick up the body, it was already gone. When all the facts were uncovered, it caused chaos and anger. In the end, the body was taken from the funeral parlor in Newark to the one in Kearny. That same night, Harry noticed that a bag of silver coins that belonged to Catherine was missing. The family was convinced that Lisa had taken the coins. With tempers at an all-time high, it looked like World War III was about to happen.

Throughout her life, Catherine was always a peacemaker. When fighting broke out between her kids, or the kids and Harry, it was Catherine who cooled things down and brought the fighting to a halt.

That evening I tried to get some sleep. With all this anger, mistrust, and sorrow going on, my mind was racing at one hundred miles per hour. It took hours before I could finally fall asleep. Around 2 AM I awakened. I looked at the foot of the bed and saw the image of Catherine. She raised her finger to her lips as if to say, *don't say a word*. She pointed her finger into the dark where mentally I saw the inside of her bedroom. The next thing I saw was the closet in the room. The door slowly opened, and I saw a row of clothes extending from one end of the closet to the other. She pointed to the steam pipe located in the corner of the closet, then ran her finger down to the base of it, then faded out.

The next morning, I told Sue about my vision of her mother. Sue picked up the phone and called her dad. She asked him to put the phone down and look in the closet. "Follow the steam pipe to the floor," she said. "Tell me if there is anything there?"

Harry came back to the phone and told her that he found the bag of coins. Lisa had not taken it after all. Once again, thanks to Catherine, all the anger between the family members dissolved.

Catherine in death made the effort to return to the living to exonerate Lisa of any wrongdoing. Catherine continued to do in death what she did in life—be a true ambassador of good will. I am glad that through my psychic ability I was there to help.

These were just a few examples of life after life. During one of my public presentations, I was asked by an elderly gent, "Is there life after death?" I quickly responded, "Yes." If those who pass can show up and tell me where to find missing money, or to curse out an old business acquaintance, the answer to the question has to be yes.

On another matter, many people believe that the dead haunt or linger around cemeteries where they are buried, and paranormal investigators spend a lot of time in such places trying to contact the dead or capture ghostly photographs and voices. I never found a cemetery to be haunted. What I do see are images of the living that were present at burials.

On occasion, I visit my relatives' graves, which are all close to my home. During one of these visits to the Holy Cross Cemetery in North Arlington, I had a startling vision. I was walking away from my Uncle Ed's grave and happened to look up from the path leading to the street. I saw about two dozen well-dressed mourners gathering in front of a small family mausoleum, and a 1930s black Cadillac hearse. The two doors of the mausoleum were wide open. A priest standing in the opening began reading from his prayer book. I could not see the deceased, but instead looked into the faces of the funeral crowd. I realized it was a vision of the past, but it looked real to me.

I was certain that those I saw were all no longer with us. It was almost like watching a film of a funeral that took place many, many years ago, where everyone in the film has since died. In my case, however, I was watching and hearing in real-time—and I was part of the show.

I walked toward the mausoleum. The images, strong and life-like, faded the closer I got, and then vanished altogether. I peeked through the glass doors and saw the death year of 1934 for this individual, confirming the time period I had guessed based on the hearse and the clothing.

Viewing something like this often leaves me feeling sad. For example, when I witnessed the people who were attending that 1934 funeral, I was looking into the faces of people who are also dead, with the exception, perhaps, of some of the children. It was an unsettling feeling. Those faces are still as clear to me as if living people were standing in front of me.

Yet, there are extraordinary benefits in having this ability. Sometimes I am privileged to witness significant events in history. In the Mount Pleasant Cemetery in Newark is the grave of Thomas Edison's first wife, Mary Stilwell. Mary was born in Newark in 1855, and at age sixteen went to work at one of Edison's subsidiaries, the News Reporting Telegraph Company. She caught his attention, and they married in 1871 when Edison was twenty-four. Lore has it that he was so engrossed in his work that he went back to his laboratory after the wedding and left his bride waiting at home until the wee hours of the night. Nonetheless, they had three children. In 1884, when Mary was twenty-nine, she was stricken with typhoid fever and died.

I have visited Mary's grave many times and have stood at various spots around it. I have watched a young Thomas Edison surrounded by many mourners. The crowd is always massive, though unfortunately I cannot recognize those around him. I am sure there are politicians, co-workers, family members, and, of course, the general public, all wanting a chance to see this amazing man even under sad circumstances.

I'll end with these thoughts:

Do everything you can in life to keep your affairs and relationships in good working order, so that when it comes time to make your transition, you leave with love and good energy. It is much more difficult to mend fences from the Other Side.

In the future mankind may find a way to conquer the element of time and have the ability to visit our past. Just think—at any event, great or ordinary, someone in the crowd may be a viewing visitor from another time, just like me.

6

The Ghost at the Lodge

Many of us have daily routines, activities, and even formal rituals that we do over and over again, and after we are gone from this earth, some of us carry on with those rituals in death.

That was the case in a poignant haunting at my Adoniram Masonic Lodge in Lyndhurst, New Jersey. It involved a departed brother who died a tragic death, and could not let go of his beloved lodge.

I became a Freemason a number of years ago, and quickly became immersed in lodge activities. I loved the history and heritage, and also the social family. I volunteered to help with the running of the lodge and organized events. My wife, Sueli, and I spent many an evening at the lodge club getting to know everyone. At first, no one at the lodge knew of my psychic abilities. Frankly, I liked it that way.

The person who is the head of the lodge and its line officers is called "The Worshipful Master." He sits in front of the room, elevated on a three-step high platform. I was the lodge historian and sat in an officer's chair on the floor to his right. From my seat, I could see each member, and I had a clear view of the two entry doors to the lodge room. At one particular meeting, shortly after I had joined the lodge, I had a startling experience. Our Worshipful Master, L. Mark Tirgrath, was presiding. Suddenly I saw the ghostly image of a brother Mason appear in front of the door, wearing his Masonic apron. I remained silent and watched as he walked to the front of the room, facing the Worshipful Master. He gave the appropriate Masonic sign of recognition and began to speak.

"Why won't you recognize me?" the ghost asked.

Mark just continued the meeting, not aware of the ghostly apparition in front of him. Apparently, I was the only person present who could see or hear this brother.

The ghost repeated, "Why won't you recognize me?" this time in a sorrowful tone. About five seconds later, he looked down, turned to his right, walked back to the door and faded out.

I sat sadly in my chair and kept quiet. Who would believe me? What would these men think of a new member making such outlandish claims of a ghost in their lodge? I knew in two weeks we would have another meeting. Would the ghost return? If he did, what should I do?

Those two weeks flew by and, once again, it was meeting night. Just like at the meeting before, I was sitting in my historian's chair, with my eyes fixed on the door.

At about 9 PM, the ghost returned. He once again walked to Mark, made the sign, and called him out by name.

"Mark, why won't you recognize me?" He lowered his head, turned to his right, walked towards the door and faded out.

This was too much for me. Keeping my ability to see the dead to myself and letting this poor soul pour his heart out to someone who ignored him was morally wrong and also wrong according to Masonic teachings. I decided to tell Mark about these ghostly visits in hopes that he would understand. When the meeting was over, I stayed behind and approached Mark to tell him of my paranormal abilities and what I witnessed. I could tell by his lukewarm reaction to my story that he probably had serious questions of my sanity, but I am sure he could see that my sincerity was genuine, so he gave me the benefit of doubt.

Adoniram Lodge in Lyndhurst, New Jersey

I called him a few days later, and we agreed to meet at the Masonic Club, also in Lyndhurst. He brought a photo of lodge officers that had been taken a few years before.

"Do you see him here?" asked Mark pointing to the picture. "Yes," I answered, and pointed to a man in the third row. I could tell it struck a nerve with Mark, and it marked a turning point in our relationship. Of all the men in the photograph, why did I pick his friend, Ed? Was it by chance or could it be what I saw in the lodge was genuine?

"That's Ed Reynolds," Mark said. "He was our lodge secretary." Mark hesitated for a few seconds. Then with a sad tone to his voice, he said, "He accidentally froze to death in his driveway a few years back. He suffered from Alzheimer's disease. We believe he was looking for his cat during a snowstorm, slipped, and laid on the ground until he died. He was a good friend of mine."

I could tell that Mark was upset, and recalling this incident hurt him emotionally. There was nothing more I could say. Mark kindly offered to buy me a drink, but I felt it was time to leave. We shook hands and before I left, Mark told me that if Ed's ghost returned at the next meeting, to let him know while the meeting was going on. I agreed to do so. Maybe with my help, we could find out why Ed was appearing at the lodge and possibly find a solution that would allow our Masonic Brother to finally rest in peace.

Then something strange happened—Ed disappeared. A few more meetings came and went, but there was no sign of him.

I stopped by the lodge one afternoon and felt something telling me to look in the attic. At the time, the attic was full of boxes, decorations, wheelchairs, walkers, and various items usually found in a Masonic Lodge. I opened the door and looked on the floor, and before me was what looked like an attaché case. I picked it up, and etched in gold lettering on the case was the name "Edward Reynolds." I opened the case and found his officer's apron, neatly placed inside. Was it Ed himself who prompted me to look in the attic? Perhaps he knew I could see and hear him at the meetings, and he was reaching out to me for help.

I immediately called Mark and told him what I had found. He rushed to the lodge. Mark was convinced that this was a gift from Ed to him and decided to wear Ed's apron from then on. Mark felt that wearing this apron would be a way to respect and honor his good friend.

But what about Ed? Would he ever return? And if so, when?

One night, I got a call from Mark. He asked if I would meet him at the lodge and call out to Ed to see if he would return. It was cold and rainy, but I agreed, and headed directly to the lodge. Mark sat down in his chair and I stood in the center of the room. I told Mark to call out Ed's name and talk to him as if he was in the room.

Mark called out, "Ed! Ed, I'd like to see you. We were good friends, and I miss you."

I stayed focused on the door, which we had left open. Mark continued calling to Ed, over and over. He looked up at the ceiling while I watched the door.

Suddenly, I could see Ed walk into the room—but this time it was different. He had become visible—not just visible to me, but solid enough so anyone could see him! I waved my arms, getting Mark's attention, pointing to the door.

Reenactment of the appearance of the ghost of Ed Reynolds

Now Mark could see Ed, too, as he walked to the center of the room. Mark momentarily stopped talking and I quickly urged him to continue. Mark began talking again and walked towards Ed. When he got about ten feet from him, the image of Ed faded out.

Mark seemed to be in a state of shock to see for himself what I had seen at the meetings. He became a true believer after that. Whenever people would say to me that they did not believe in ghosts, Mark would jump right in and tell them about his ghostly encounter.

But this was not the last we heard of Ed.

In the months that followed, our lodge was in the midst of a fight with another lodge that was meeting in our building. Tempers flared and harsh words were thrown back and forth at meetings and social gatherings as members of each lodge aired their complaints and accusations. Ed did not like this. Of those who knew his character, they all agreed that this behavior in his lodge would be very disturbing to him.

Apparently, Ed decided to do something about it. Soon, anytime a meeting was going on, we could hear someone or something running in the attic above the lodge room, back and forth, as if to get our attention. If it wasn't in the attic, we could hear running up and down the stairs from the first floor to the second. Up and down, up and down.

The sound of someone running was so loud that, on a few occasions when I acted as the "Tyler," the one who guards outside the door, I checked the hall and the basement gathering room to see if someone had entered the building. Of course, no "living" person had entered.

When the troubles within the lodge ended, so did the visitations by Ed, but we still have unusual things occurring at the lodge. The organ in the lodge room sometimes plays music by itself, but when anyone tries to reach the organ and gets within a few feet of the door, the music stops. There also are instances when a lodge member who is alone in the building hears the organ playing.

We have had objects disappear and reappear. One of our members, Mike Paserchia, was helping out with some construction work in the building when his jacket vanished. He had placed it on one of the chairs in the lodge room, and in a few minutes, it was missing. A handful of members who were there that day searched the building from cellar to attic, in closets and drawers, but the jacket was not found.

The following week, I went into the attic to put away a box of light bulbs. When I opened the door to the crawl space, there was Mike's jacket, staring at me in the face. We had checked this place a week earlier, and the jacket wasn't there!

Mark Tirgrath with Ed Reynolds' apron

On Saturdays, the officers of the lodge meet to practice their Masonic rituals for degrees. Freemasonry is based on many rituals that must be performed exactly and perfectly. The words spoken must not deviate from the written word, and the footwork by the participants must also be flawless. The District Deputy represents the Grand Lodge of the State and will, at various times during the year, critique the lodge's ability to perform its rituals, making sure they are up to the standards set by the Grand Lodge. Lodges that fail to meet these expectations are penalized, and an intense effort is made to bring their rituals to an acceptable performance.

On this one particular Saturday I, along with the other officers, were at the lodge practicing for an upcoming degree. Former Worshipful Master Jimmy Lind guided us step by step through the rituals, often referring to his Masonic ritual book, which he always held in his hand. When practice was over, everyone left the building. Jimmy was well on his way home before he remembered that he forgot his ritual book on the banister post in the hall next to the front door. He immediately called me to return to the lodge to retrieve the book. I live only a few miles away and could be there in a matter of minutes.

I went to the lodge, but the book was not there. I searched the entire building, and his book could not be found. I did find a ritual book in the attic storeroom, but it was new and lacked Jimmy's hand written notations he had made over the years—something that made his personal book priceless.

Later that week, I stopped by the lodge to bring in the mail. It was Wednesday and I wanted to make sure the lodge was ready for our meeting that night. I unlocked the front door, and when I stepped inside, Jimmy's ritual book was on the banister post, exactly where he said he had left it on Saturday. I had to wonder, was it Ed, or maybe someone else from the other side, having a laugh at our expense? Or, were these stunts directed at me? Were spirits trying to tell me that they controlled the situation at the lodge, and not me?

When these strange things were happening at the lodge, most of the younger Masons were convinced that Ed was responsible. The older members, with only a few exceptions, had no opinion or disregarded these actions as nonsense. That did not surprise me. Those with closed minds will come up with ridiculous explanations for paranormal phenomena. They will pass something off as a prank, coincidence, "vibrations," or the most common excuse of them all, "It didn't happen, you just imagined it."

Haunted Masonic Lodges are not rare. As a matter of fact, you will find lists of Masonic Lodges throughout the world that claim to be haunted. Paranormal researcher George Hansen has a theory about this. When someone performs the same actions over and over, such as what Freemasons do in their rituals, some of these people, even after death, will continue to perform their rituals. This theory, which I firmly believe, explains the reason behind the high number of haunted lodges.

I feel the spirit of Ed will remain at the Adoniram Lodge. I was told that when he was alive, Ed always looked out for the lodge, and that it was the most important thing in his life. As long as the lodge exists, I am convinced that Ed will remain there, watching over it.

7

Do Not Forget Me!

No one wants to be forgotten, even in death, as the Daisy and Ed stories so poignantly reveal. Sometimes just a single photograph or memento keeps a memory alive. This case, in which the dead reached out to me to save their memory, was unusual for two reasons: The dead person spoke only to me and no one else; and, I had no visual impression. Usually my contact with the dead involves both voice and mental image, but this one was vision-free.

This investigation took me outside of my usual urban settings to the small town of Island Heights on the Jersey shore. The town—literally on an island—had its beginnings on July 1, 1878, when the Island Heights Association, started by a Methodist Church group, purchased one hundred seventy-two acres of land. On it they built a campground, pavilion, thirty cottages, and a wharf to help transport people to and from the island on the river. In 1975 the Borough of Island Heights purchased the property and converted many of the buildings to municipality usage, and kept some sites for recreation.

Many of the old cottages were torn down over the years. A few remained, only slightly changed from their nineteenth-century construction. One such house is the center of this story. What made this particular house special was that its owner, Carol Bedford, was convinced that this house was haunted.

Carol had gone on a skiing trip with a group of friends, and during the course of social conversation, confided her suspicions about the house. She asked her friends if they knew any "ghost hunter" who could confirm the haunting and get rid of the ghost. My cousin, Diana Sulewski, happened to be on the trip and was intrigued by Carol's story. She told Carol that her cousin Karl dealt with ghosts and hauntings, and that he would be the person to contact.

A few weeks later, I received a phone call from Carol. She seemed very sincere and concerned about her "ghostly" situation. During our conversation, she told me that she and her husband bought this particular house as a get-away for their large family. The location was great because it had easy access to the seashore. She said the house was quite old, and each room had dark stained wood on the walls and most of the ceilings—a feature that would prove to be important in the haunting.

At the end of our conversation, I agreed to visit the house. I made no other promises to her about what I might discover, or what I could do. I had never heard of Island Heights, nor had any of my friends whom I queried.

A week later, I set out with my paranormal sidekick, Christine Hague. I printed out the driving directions from my computer, picked up Christine, and we were off. It took us about an hour to arrive at the exit off the Garden State Parkway and onto the adjacent local highway. After a few miles, we made a right turn off the highway and onto a side road which took us up a steep hill; at the top was a great panoramic view of Toms River below. We started down the hill and after a few turns, found ourselves at the Bedford house.

We were the first ones to arrive, so I grabbed my camera and took pictures of the outside of the house and property. Christine watched from the truck as I snapped picture after picture. By the time I finished three sides of the building, I had an opinion that this old building had major structural issues. Over the years, the many owners and tenants clearly had not invested any significant money to make the house more livable or to beautify it. The building had an overall look of being tired.

When I finished taking photos, I returned to my truck where Christine was waiting. I opened the tailgate and started to assemble my video camera and tripod. I said to Christine, "There's no doubt that there is an entity in this house, not only can I feel it, I can hear a woman's voice inside the house trying to speak to me."

The haunted house in Island Heights, New Jersey

Just as I finished putting the battery into the camera, Carol arrived. She was a sharp individual, not the type to imagine things or blow things out of proportion in order to get attention.

We gathered across the narrow street to observe the house. As I placed my tripod with the camera on the ground, I asked, "Don't you feel like someone is watching you from the second floor window?"

With a look of surprise, Carol answered, "Yes, I do."

I stepped out a few feet, then I turned and faced Carol and Christine with my back to the building. I said, "We are being watched by an entity on the second floor right now. Before either of them could reply, I added, "When I walked around the house, I could sense it watching me. It was moving from room to room, looking out each window."

Carol said she felt someone was always watching her, which gave her an eerie, sickening feeling. Her kids keep telling her that the place was "creepy" and they did not want to be there. Her dog refused to go to the second floor, but would stand at the foot of the stairs and whimper while looking up the staircase.

I told Carol that the voice I heard in my mind earlier was getting louder. It was the voice of a woman saying, "The boys are coming in today, on the train," and then, "The boys will soon be here."

I asked Carol if there was a train station in town. She replied that train service to Island Heights had ended more than eighty years ago. When the church controlled this area, a man named John Wanamaker, founder of the Wanamaker department store in Philadelphia, used Island Heights as a summer retreat for his workers. That was one of the reasons the trains came in from Philadelphia daily at that time.

The voice I was hearing that came in so clear suddenly was getting softer and softer until it was so low that it was impossible to hear. It was like a battery in a tape recorder getting weaker. To continue this investigation would have been a wasted effort, so I asked Carol if we could come back in about a month to try again. Carol agreed, so we said our goodbyes and drove off. In my rear view mirror, I watched Carol returning to the house to lock up.

During the trip back home, Christine and I exchanged thoughts about what we had seen and felt. Christine said that while we were still on the property; she had heard the woman's voice, too. Her description of the voice and what it said matched my experience. This is not unusual, for often when people accompany me on an investigation or inspection, they will experience some of the same paranormal anomalies that I do. However, their visions and feelings disappear in a short time, and mine stay with me for days or longer.

I spent many nights thinking about this mystery. I searched the internet and read anything I could find about Island Heights. I had a feeling that something in the town's history needed to be brought to light. Through all these efforts, I found no answers or reasons for what was happening at this house. Carol told me that during those religious camp days back in the 1800s, her house was used as the camp office where visitors would register for their stays.

About five weeks went by before Christine and I returned. Before I made my final turn into the street, I heard the voice again, and this time it was stronger. Carol was already at the house and greeted us as we drove up.

Just as I walked into the kitchen, the voice clearly said, "It's in the wood." Then it repeated, "It's in the wood, look in the wood."

I walked through each room on the first floor, pressing on the walls and ceilings while the voice of the woman continued its mantra, "It's in the wood" with each and every step. Carol followed me with a small camcorder. I must have looked like a raging maniac banging on the walls in every room. What was in the wood? What was meant by "It's in the wood"?

Christine touched every board she could get her hands on while both of us were being observed by the watchful eye of Carol's camera. I didn't mind being recorded, and in fact thought that it would demonstrate what I do and the lengths I will go to during an investigation. If I cracked my head on a board or fell through the floor, Carol's video would have to be edited because of the audio comment I would have made.

When I finished pressing on every board on the first floor, I turned my attention to the second floor. As I was moving up the stairs, the voice got louder. Room by room, I pressed, tugged and pulled on every board, but the dark wainscoting surrendered nothing.

I noticed as I walked by the ladder to the attic that the voice got stronger. I walked up the ladder to the attic and found myself looking into a big black space void of any lights. I looked at the floor beams and saw they were made of two-by-threes, which by today's building standard are unacceptable because they lack the strength to hold up the ceilings or flooring.

Nevertheless, I decided to crawl across the attic beams. By crawling, my weight would be dispersed across many of the beams, thus avoiding the risk of dropping through the attic floor and ending up on the second floor, probably on my back, looking up at a big hole in the ceiling.

As I inched across the attic floor, the voice took on a tone of urgency, becoming so loud in my head that it was deafening: "In the wood, in the wood!" The voice literally went from a whisper to a scream. At the height of the screaming, I put my right hand alongside one of the wall beams, and my fingers touched a piece of metal. The voice instantly stopped.

The metal was loose, and I carefully pulled it up. I had a small flashlight on my keychain, and shined the light on the metal. It was a piece of tin with a black gloss on one side. When I turned it over, I was astonished to see a black-and-white photograph of a young woman in period clothing wearing a large cross around her neck. This tin picture appeared to be more than a century old, yet it was in perfect condition.

Tintype of the mystery woman

I brought the tintype down from the attic. As my foot hit the floor, the house felt different to me—a calm permeated the rooms. Christine felt it immediately as well, and so did Carol. I knew that the woman's voice belonged to the woman in the photograph, and she had directed me to find it.

A thought went through my mind. I said to Carol, "Did you ever say to your husband that you were planning on tearing down this house?"

"Yes," said Carol. She acknowledged that the house was in such poor condition that bringing it up to code would cost more than tearing it down and building something new.

"Did you have this conversation, in this house?" I asked.

"Yes," she answered again. "No wonder she was haunting this place."

There was no name on the photo. Whoever this woman was, she evidently was attached to this house. It was her ghost that looked out the windows and monitored each person that came around or into the house. She sat in on all the conversations of the guests in *her* house.

It was clear to me that she had eavesdropped on the conversation between Carol and her husband regarding their plans to level the house. For some reason, that tin picture had been placed in the attic, probably a long time ago, and only the ghost knew why or how it got there. The picture could have been a keepsake that she had given to a loved one. Without rescue, this treasure of the woman's memory, all wrapped up in one tin photo, would have been destroyed by a crew of hardhat workers tearing down this old building to make way for a new one.

This is not the first time I had discovered a ghost haunting a home or building because it feared being forgotten. For more than a century, this woman had waited patiently for her picture to be found. How many people did she speak to in vain because they could not hear her voice?

I was happy that her wait was finally over. Now that her picture was rescued from the wrecking ball, it could be displayed either in Carol's house or even the historical society of the town. I doubt we will ever know the identity of the woman, but her beautiful image on tin will be preserved for many years to come, and her memory will live on.

The haunting problems ceased the moment the picture was found and did not return.

One of the most important requests of the dead is, "Do not forget me." Yet, in our fast-paced Western culture, we all too often let the dead fade away. We bury our dead, and, as time goes by, visit the graves less and less, and get out the photos and mementoes less and less—or even sell them or throw them away. Many other cultures have long-standing traditions for honoring the dead and keeping their memories alive. There is a vital link between the world of the living and the dead in the afterlife. We would be wise to nourish it.

8

The Pitfalls of Ghost Hunting

As you can see from the cases I have related thus far, I take paranormal investigations quite seriously. The spirit I have been asked to contact could be the lost soul of someone's mother, father, sister, brother, grandfather, grandmother, or dear friend. I am often the only instrument that links our reality with theirs, and their situations are often quite sensitive. When I take on that responsibility, I will not stand in front of that spirit holding a camera or some electronic device just to prove to others what transpired between me and them. You can call it my personal ethics.

You may wonder, why not try to capture the spirit in a photo or video? Popular ghost hunting television shows emphasize the collection of evidence, and feature people acting out when they think a spirit is around them. Most of these shows are not real investigations, but entertainment, and what you see on the screen may not be what really happened. Investigators do capture plenty of unexplained photos and videos, but unfortunately there is also a great deal of hoaxing and fraud, thanks to software that makes it easy to fabricate and embellish images. Hoaxed "ghost photographs" circulate on the internet all the time.

If I was fortunate enough to capture a photo of an apparition and I put it on public display, I would likely have a multitude of doubters claim that I fabricated the photo. These people would consider me a fraud, and it would cloud both my credibility as an investigator and my reputation as a psychic.

These same doubters might also demand that I provide proof by taking them to the site so they could witness the paranormal phenomena firsthand. Phenomena do not manifest on cue, however; there are a host of unknown conditions that contribute to a manifestation.

Even if I was lucky and the phenomena they came to see did happen right in front of them, they probably still would not believe. If nothing happens on cue, I remain a fraud in their eyes, so I lose either way—the hardline skeptics would say that I somehow fabricated the whole thing. If not fraud, their accusations might be that I was mistaken, gullible, or naive. So, photos, eyewitnesses, audio recordings, and other types of "proof" are essentially worthless in the eyes of skeptics. No wonder many people keep quiet about their experiences and even evidence.

You may have the impression that I am against the use of electronic equipment. Not at all. Those individuals or groups who like to use them in paranormal investigations have my blessings. I get my information through psychic means; they do not. If equipment does produce evidence, I can psychically validate it. The experiment with the ghost box in the Daisy case is an example. We were attempting to get more information in addition to what I had already learned.

George Hansen, a respected researcher in the field, emphasizes that "phenomena do not happen on demand," and I agree. Ghostly phenomena may happen at various locations on various days and at various times. Just because I may decide to stop at a "hot spot" of activity to investigate, that doesn't mean anything will show itself to me. I may have to return again and again, possibly over long periods of time, before a spirit makes itself known to me—or maybe it never will.

Rosemary Ellen Guiley, one of the leading researchers and investigators of the paranormal, agrees. "The manifestation of any phenomena—visual, voice, or physical—depends on many variables," she said. "Factors such as day or night, season, weather and atmospheric conditions, and even lunar phases can play a role. The biggest wild card of all is human consciousness. Some people seem to stimulate or trigger phenomena, and others can actually depress it, all unwittingly. There may be something generated in their energy fields or consciousness that interacts in certain ways with the energies that make manifestation possible. Groups of people form collective energy fields, or thought-forms, that also can have an impact.

"I have done many multiple investigations of the same active sites, and have also investigated some sites over long periods of time. There is rarely, if ever, an exact duplication of phenomena. You may get similar things happening repetitively, but not in exactly the same way. It is not unusual to have nothing happen, even though activity took place at another time. All of these variables, combined with the subjective nature of personal perception, make it difficult for investigators to "prove" anything in a way that would be acceptable to science. We do have a great deal of evidence 'in support of' the paranormal, but it will never satisfy the hardcore critics."

Others who do genuine investigations have similar points of view. Yet, television entertainment conveys to the public that ghosts and phenomena happen all the time, and in very dramatic ways, especially whenever an "investigation" takes place. It would not be exciting to watch a show where investigators sat around in the dark all night and nothing happened. They have to deliver to keep the ratings up. Don't get me wrong, sometimes genuine phenomena do happen in the course of TV show investigations. We just need to keep in mind that paranormal entertainment is not always an accurate portrayal.

Another point I would like to address concerns people who are terrified of the supernatural, but cover it up with false bravado. Some people who have fears of the paranormal avoid it altogether, but others, mostly men, become a self-proclaimed "voice of reason" and loudly challenge everything and everybody connected with investigations. You will find them joking at the most inappropriate times, and professing knowledge of things about which they really know nothing.

A good example is the story of Dan. Dan is a member of my Masonic Lodge. He is a kind and generous man, and it was Dan who introduced me to Masonry. He is an avid reader, and has a strong interest in esoteric literature. He is very knowledgeable on these subjects and is always willing to partake in a conversation or a debate. At various times he has heard my conversations or talks about my paranormal investigations. He always starts laughing and interrupts my talk, saying that he wants to see a ghost. He jokes that he wants to bring a six-pack of beer and share it with the ghost. Dan has insisted that I bring him along to an investigation to *prove* to him that ghosts exist!

I am not a missionary, and it is not my mission in life to prove the existence of ghosts to anyone. Should I bring someone with me to an investigation, it will not be a person who wants to be entertained. There is nothing I can do, show, or say that will satisfy someone like Dan. They will just go away grumpy and more convinced than ever that ghosts and the paranormal do not exist.

For the record, no one can prove the existence of ghosts to a legal degree, just as it is impossible for a priest, rabbi, or minister to prove to a legal degree the existence of God. Some things in life are plainly and simply faith-based. Before I decide to take on an investigation, I take into consideration the circumstances surrounding the paranormal incident and the credibility of the witnesses. As I mentioned before, I will always bring *someone* to accompany me on my investigations. In the past, it has been Dr. Joanne D.S. McMahon, Rosemary Ellen Guiley, or Christine Hague. There have been others over the years—too many to mention by name. I don't mind sharing my investigations with others, but I do have criteria. When someone says to me that he or she is "open-minded" but "skeptical," that is a sign that this person is really closed-minded.

This is how I operate during my investigations: if an apparition should appear in the room with me, or if an object should move across a table or the floor, I quietly witness the event and patiently wait to see if "it" will try to make contact with me, either verbally or mentally. However, the "open minded skeptics" will shout out, make noises, and turn to me to question if it was some sort of a trick perpetrated on them by me. These outbursts hinder the investigation to such a degree that everyone might as well go home.

Here is a good example. After the terror attacks on the World Trade Center in New York City in 2001, I purposely avoided going to ground zero for years. I did not know what to expect and feared that many of the dead were still there, and I might not be able to handle a multitude of entities on such a grand level. Being overly sensitive, I could have easily become psychically overwhelmed. I discussed this problem with Rosemary and she convinced me to give it a try. She was visiting me at the time with a friend, Greg. Rosemary is an asset in any type of investigation. She knows what and what not to do in response to any developments. I was uncertain about Greg, whom I did not know well, and who seemed to want to prove his own abilities in a loud way.

It was late on a Sunday night when Rosemary, Greg, Sue, and I drove to ground zero. We parked on one of the side streets near the site and walked close to the base of what had been World Trade Center I. There was still a huge gash in the earth, and reconstruction efforts were underway.

I told everyone to stay at least twenty feet behind me, and that if I saw something I would tell them what I was experiencing. Minutes later I observed at the end of the block what appeared to be a large bar code that extended across the entire width of the street. The bars were shaking and bending as they were approaching me,

I called out what I was experiencing, in seconds those bars turned into people—office people. In front was a large man wearing a white shirt with his sleeves rolled up past his elbows. I stopped and just watched as these images approached me. I turned half way around and motioned to the others to stop and stay well behind me. The faces were becoming very clear, and I felt I would have psychic contact in a few moments. These people seemed to be stuck and lost, perhaps from the shock of the event. It was a delicate moment, and I needed to hold the energy. I knew they could see me, and my impression was that they were approaching me for help.

Just as these images were almost next to me, Greg ran in front of me and yelled, "I see them, too!" It was as if someone hit a switch. The images and psychic feelings disappeared. Everything— all the souls—vanished. I could not reconnect. The experience was ruined and the opportunity wasted. I should have known better to include someone like Greg. I have no one to blame but myself.

In the past, I have been asked to work with participants who use their various ghost-detecting "gadgets." The constant focus on equipment was distracting and hindered the effectiveness of my psychic ability. If it wasn't the ghost gear, it was a cell phone going off at the worst time. In a darkened room, the glow of a phone visually wrecks my concentration. To many, "ghost hunting" is nothing more than a fun evening out. Their mission is to try to get scared so they can tell ghost stories to their friends. They do not take these investigations seriously.

George Hansen encountered this mindset when he once gave a talk to a ghost-hunting group in Westfield, New Jersey. He encouraged the group to become more professional, to record their research and findings, cut out articles they found on the subject from newspapers, journals, and magazines, and catalogue their photos, videos, and audio recordings. I videotaped his talk, but avoided showing the listening audience. From the looks on their faces, most were bored to tears, and I overheard comments that this was just a waste of time. Instead of listening to George, they could have been scaring themselves out in some graveyard, snapping away with their cameras and lining the ground with microphones trying to get their ghostly answers to questions on their recording equipment.

I have also seen "investigations" that are little more than excuses for food fests. The first things to come out of the trucks are big bins of snacks and drinks, pizzas, and even deep fat fryers for fries and meat. Many of the investigators spend most of the night huddled around the food.

Give me a hand-picked, select crew of one or two people, a place known for paranormal activity, and the time to do a thorough investigation, and we will stand a good chance of getting results. Many times the "ghost sightings" are actually the imprints of images from the past that often confuse people into thinking they are actual ghosts. These "imprints" are common, and are even a relief to some who fear ghosts. Yet others who want "real" ghosts are disappointed by imprints.

When my investigations conclude, there is no fanfare, no hoopla, and no "high fives." We just thank the families, tell them our findings, and quietly leave. We may take a few pictures of the house or a video that shows where the phenomena happened. I often keep these as part of my personal records. As I mentioned before, photos or videos we take are never used to "prove" the existence of an entity.

I do not want you to get the impression that I am the only person who can conduct a meaningful paranormal investigation— there are many paranormal investigators who are marvelous. Rick Fisher, from Columbia, Pennsylvania, is the President of the Paranormal Society of Pennsylvania, and is one such paranormal investigator I take seriously.

Rick will be the first to tell you the time it takes him to conduct a meaningful investigation, and it is never just a single day or even a single weekend. For example, in his research of Bube's Brewery in Mt. Joy, Pennsylvania, it took months before he captured voices in an EVP (Electronic Voice Phenomena) recording. Over the years, Rick has recorded hundreds of voices at many locations, yet he acknowledges that he does not believe that most of the voices recorded are of a ghostly origin.

On the other side of the spectrum is my good friend and psychic, Paula Roberts. One of my favorite stories about her is when she was featured on an episode of the TV show *Unsolved Mysteries*, hosted by the actor Robert Stack. In the episode, Paula was taken to the General Wayne Inn, near Philadelphia, to investigate the inn's reports of ghosts.

The inn had been the scene of violence and tragedy. In 1995 it was acquired by two men, Jim Webb and Guy Sileo, who had a rocky partnership in running the inn and restaurant. When their financial fortunes took a downward turn, Webb—who had a controlling interest—was leaning toward closing the establishment.

In 1996, Webb was found murdered in his upstairs office at the inn. He had been shot by Sileo for life insurance money, and to prevent Webb from closing the inn. During the criminal investigation, Felicia Moyse, a twenty-year-old assistant chef at the inn, committed suicide on February 22, 1997, perhaps due to knowledge about the crime. Sileo was convicted and sentenced to life in prison. The inn was sold in 2005 and is now a synagogue and center for Jewish life.

Violent death often leaves imprints, and many people reported paranormal activity at the inn. When Paula visited for the show, she pointed out where the ghosts were often seen, and she accurately described what these ghosts looked like—all of which corroborated the reports of eye witnesses.

Paula is extremely accurate, and I always find her a joy to work with. Like me, Paula does not use any electrical or mechanical devices to track entities. She uses her innate psychic abilities. We both frown on people who yell and scream at the slightest noise during an investigation. When I am asked to recommend a psychic for a reading, without a second thought, I recommend Paula, "The English Psychic." It must be due to her British "reserve" that, during an investigation, when things happen that would scare most people, she takes it all in stride.

Many ghost hunts and investigations are interesting and worthwhile activities, and are organized and led by knowledgeable investigators. The quality varies considerably. Some paranormal groups have events that are open to the public. If you have never been on an investigation and are curious about them, you will have an easy time finding one in your area. It is one way to learn some of the basics. Keep in mind that most of the action will not register on equipment, but on your own sensitivity.

My thoughts on paranormal investigations are:

Whenever you are involved with seeking or communicating with the spirits of the dead, give them the respect they deserve and do not treat your investigation as a substitute for a night of bowling.

9

The Psychic Television Show

In the previous chapter, I talked about how paranormal investigation is often turned into entertainment. Well, sometimes the entertainment is me, the psychic.

It is unfortunate that a true psychic does not have a switch built into his body that can control his psychic force so that he can turn it on when he wants to use it and just "hit-the-switch" to turn it off when it is time to relax. Well, I can tell you that psychics would love to have such a device, but sadly, it has not been invented.

The story I am about to tell shows the trials and tribulations of how a typical night for a psychic can start out fine, but much too often, can end on an unsettling note. Sometimes I am put in the uncomfortable position of revealing my ability, at the risk of having others criticize or reject me.

The following is what happened when my wife Sue and I decided to have a night out with friends.

On a Saturday evening, we joined our friends Harold and his wife, Sharon, for dinner. Harold, like Sue, is a psychologist, and they work together at the same hospital in Newark. This was a first-time visit to this combination Brazilian Rodizio/Sushi restaurant for all of us. As we drove past the restaurant, we could see that the inside was mobbed with people. After circling the building for the third time, hoping for someone to free up a parking space, we lucked out and got a spot near the front door. Once we passed the huge, glass entry doors, we were greeted by the hostess, who confirmed our reservation. We were taken to a table and waited a few minutes until Harold and Sharon showed. The dining rooms were dimly lit and decorated with a motif of red walls and modernistic chrome sconces. The speakers built into the ceiling were blasting techno rock music at the level where table conversation became close to impossible.

After our friends arrived, Harold and Sue began a high-volume chat regarding some of the changes being made at the hospital where they both worked, and how these changes would affect their jobs. Sharon and I, sitting just a couple of feet away, could catch only a few words here and there, due to the non-stop thumping of the mind-numbing music.

At a Brazilian Rodizio, you first help yourself to an enormous salad bar. Then waiters periodically stop by your table with a skewer of various meats and slide off pieces of whatever you want. These meat visitations happen all night, until you post a "no-more-meat" flag on your table. Take it from me: you won't find a vegetarian at a Brazilian Rodizio!

Harold and Sharon knew nothing about my psychic abilities. Whenever I was included in the conversation, I kept the talk light and non-controversial. "How's work?" or "Are you into sports?" are usually safe conversation-starters people use at dinners. I'll do my share of chit chat and make the best of small talk, but it's not the time to say to someone, "By the way, I'm a psychic." That's not the icebreaker you want for starting a conversation. Once you make a statement like that, send home the piano player, the magician and the clown, because you have just become the entertainment for the evening or, even worse, you are now "the weirdo sitting at our table."

People think of a psychic as a person who can tell their future by reading palms or gazing into a crystal ball. Once I make it known that I am a psychic, all those around me will insist that I reveal to them their future lovers, career opportunities and, while I'm at it, the winning lottery numbers for the next day. If I decline to do the "dog-and-pony show" for the crowd, I'll be the most hated person in the room—and I can forget about ever being invited to another night out with those people. Knowing the risk, I keep my psychic-self deep under wraps. In public, I try my best to blend in with the people around me. I can put up a convincing façade, but that does not guarantee that an entire evening will run smoothly. At times, an uncontrollable paranormal occurrence will happen to me. Of course, one of those uncontrollable events had to happen on *this* evening with friends who knew nothing about the "real" me.

When a paranormal episode starts for me, I sense the room taking on a different *feel*. I am no stranger to this effect, and I know exactly what is happening and how it will progress. It always starts with a small ringing in my ears. Next, the movement of people around me starts to slow down, and then the noise of the crowd begins to subside. I can clearly see psychic images surrounding each individual, as if each one has a small television over his right shoulder. These images show events from the person's past, especially those that hurt him emotionally. A few seconds later, I get insights into his character, and within the space of a few minutes, these fleeting images are in full force. Once this shift starts, there is nothing I can do to stop it. Everything has to run its course.

On this occasion, this shift began about half-way through the meal. I glanced around at the other tables. I lifted my head, focusing my eyes on a woman at the next table. She was in her mid-to-late twenties. She was dressed elegantly, had long blonde hair, perfect makeup, and glowing jewelry wrapped around her neck and wrist. I knew she was on a date and was trying desperately to impress her man by being charming and witty. Images of this woman kept flashing in my mind at a high rate of speed. I knew that this was not her first date with this man, but probably her third. I could also see that she had recently been romantically involved with another man. Plans for marriage had been made, but things had fallen apart, leaving her devastated.

The accuracy of this scenario is without question. This has happened to me so many times before that this is what I call a "given," meaning *extra high accuracy*. Over the years, whenever anyone has checked out my psychic information after an episode like this, the results have been off the scale with accuracy.

A moment later, I glanced up at the table next to the wall: more people, more images, and more input. When I receive a lot of information in such a short time, it becomes too much for me to handle. So, I immediately diverted my eyes to the top of the table—I had had enough. It was now time for me to look at the salt-and-pepper shaker and the breadcrumbs sitting alongside my plate.

"Don't look at people, *whatever* you do!" I kept saying to myself, because if I were to continue looking at people, the incoming images would develop into unbearable pain in my head, like the ultimate migraine.

The images that I usually receive from people are not happy ones. This is a characteristic of many psychic impressions, including precognition and also haunting phenomena. The negative will stand out much more than anything positive. In my experiences, the pain suffered by the people in those images is transferred to me. In short, I become an involuntary empath—someone who can actually *feel* what others are feeling, or, as is often the case, what others have *felt* in the past. It is astonishing to me how long emotional pain lingers in the energy field of a person. If we were all aware of that, I am certain we would treat each other much differently.

Harold noticed my odd behavior and asked if there was anything wrong. This was not new or a surprise to Sue. She knew quite well what was happening. She had seen this many, many times before.

Sue said, "Tell him. Go ahead. It's all right."

I hesitated for a second, then began to tell Harold and Sharon about my ability. Remember, I was seated at the table with two psychologists, so a story that would seem crazy to the general public was just another interesting adventure to Harold and Sueli. In fact, I had a rare, non-judgmental audience, and Harold was about to be introduced to a phenomenon not taught to psychologists or psychiatrists in any college or university.

For Harold and Sharon, my ability was quite odd and strange. Even with all his years of treating clients, Harold found himself on new ground. For Sharon, it was *all* weird. Most people never think beyond the mundane details and activities of daily life. Anything beyond that is off the charts, often too much to absorb.

As the evening wore on, the pounding of the techno rock music was lowered, and empty tables appeared throughout the room. I was almost finished explaining about myself when four people, three men and a woman, came in and sat at a table about ten feet away from ours. During my conversation with my dinner companions, I had kept focused on the crumbs scattered on our tabletop. Hearing new voices near us, I casually looked up to see who these people were. Since I was sitting with a psychologist who has never been exposed to someone like me, I thought it would be a perfect time to make my point about my psychic ability and how it worked.

I quietly said to Harold that two of the three men sitting together were gay and that they had all driven to the restaurant in a late-model white Audi, which was parked directly in the front of the building. Harold smiled. I was sure he thought this could not be true. How could a man sitting at this table, without seeing the outside of the building, have this information? One of the men sitting at the table leaned over and kissed the other man on the cheek. Harold did not see it, but Sharon did, and raised her eyebrow at me in confirmation.

It was getting late, so we ended the evening by talking about plans for our next get-together. We all put on our coats and walked out the front door. As we descended the stairs, we noticed that Harold was still at the top, just standing there.

"There it is," he said. "The white Audi, parked in front of the building, just like you said." Sharon quickly turned her head to see the car. Sue looked at me, wearing a slight smile as if to say, "No surprise to me!"

Were Harold and Sharon really convinced of my strange ability? I do not know, for they avoided comment. Most people, and especially those in the mental health field, tend to play it safe and rarely deviate from conventional teachings. Most do not want to risk expressing opinions or observations that are contrary to the accepted teachings of their profession.

I don't blame them. Who in his right mind would want to be confronted with controversy, especially from his colleagues? Any opinion, either pro or con, about a psychic encounter will be challenged. How does one accurately explain the unexplainable? Maybe one day the medical field will accept the existence of psychic ability. I do not believe it will be soon, however, and most likely, it will not be not in my lifetime.

Meanwhile, I have to remain true to myself, and allow my ability to help others who do believe.

10

Previewing Criminal Intent

Over the years I have been called in on many matters of death involving both natural and unnatural causes. People I have never met have asked me to determine the reason for a suicide or the whereabouts of someone who has vanished. Every case is different, and they always leave deep impressions on both my mind and soul that linger for a long time. The case itself may come to an end, but the effects of it remain with me.

The most difficult situation that I ever faced involved family members. What do you do when you know disturbing facts about a person's death, but because you arrived at these facts through psychic means, no one will take what you say seriously?

This most difficult case concerned my Uncle Stan and his wife, Anne. So that you can understand it, I'll fill in the background about the personal dynamics.

Uncle Stan was an odd character. He had a strange way of looking at life. For one thing, he was cheap. For example, once a year during the summer, he took my brother and me to the Jersey shore for a day at the beach. He began the trip by filling up the car tank with gasoline, which he bought at a creepy gas station in the seedy part of the city. They had the cheapest gas around, and if you needed oil, they had jars of used motor oil to top off your oil level for a dime. The most direct highway to the seashore was the Garden State Parkway. But, that was a toll road, and Stan would have nothing to do with paying for that. With a tank full of cheap gas, Stan took the old back roads to the shore. What should have been a quick trip always turned into a lengthy journey, all for the benefit of saving a dollar at best.

I clearly remember riding in the back seat of his 1955 Chevrolet with no air conditioning, baking in the sun, and sitting in traffic on these crowded side roads just to avoid tolls. I felt like I was in a steamy sauna.

Another example of his cheapness was how he used—or rather, did not use—electricity. If he was watching a ball game on his television and went to the bathroom, he would turn the TV off, and then turn it back on when he returned. He always said, "Why waste electricity, if no one is watching the game?"

Visiting him late in the afternoon might require sitting almost in complete darkness for a while, because he would not turn on the light until the sun was down. If you dared to turn the light on before sunset, he would quickly tell you to turn it off and point to the window to remind you of the setting sun's position.

He even had a unique technique for dispensing soda. He would buy a bargain brand of ginger ale to keep on hand. To be a good host, he would offer some and then ask if you would care for a glass. If you said yes, he would fill the glass about halfway with the ginger ale and then fill the rest of the glass with tap water.

Don't get me wrong, there were nice things about him—but it was his cheapness that stands out in the minds of all that knew him. His habits did enable him to pile up a fair amount of wealth. He was always secretive about his financial affairs, so none of us in the family knew what he really had until he was gone.

Stan's mother, Josephine, lived with him. Since both of my grandparents died before I was born, I and all the kids in our family considered Josephine to be our grandmother. When Stan's father died, his mother continued sharing the apartment with him on Pulaski Street. Later, they moved to a small, two-family house he bought on Houston Street. They lived on the second floor apartment and rented the first floor apartment to another uncle of mine, Eddie, whom I mentioned earlier was one of my favorite relatives.

In 1957, Stan married a woman named Mary. She was a nice, sweet woman who could speak Polish, which was an important factor in their relationship because Stan's mother could not speak English. Mary graciously shared the small living quarters with Stan and his mother. Unfortunately, Mary and Josephine did not get along, and fighting between them was commonplace. Often my brother Mark, my cousin Diana, and I would stop by to say hello. If we visited when the two women were fighting, the tension was unbearable. We sat at the kitchen table while Mary stared at Josephine and Josephine stared back at her. Not a word would be said between them. So much for the happy home.

This tension took a toll on Mary, who had a weak heart. She worked for years at a pharmaceutical company, then due to health reasons had to give up her job. After that, as the months passed, she became weaker and weaker. After years of doctor visits and tests, Mary died in 1966.

Once again, Uncle Stan was living alone in the apartment with his mother. He drank much more after that. In fact, most of the time he was either drunk or coming off a drunk. He constantly yelled at his mother, calling her names and threatening to send her off to a nursing home.

Miraculously, he always managed to sober up for work in the morning. To my knowledge, he never missed a day. He worked for the United States Postal Service and saved his sick days so that he had months upon months of accrued paid days available to him.

Blackberry brandy was the drink of choice for Josephine, who also over-indulged like her son. She spent a lot of her time walking up and down the stairs to the first floor and through the apartment where Uncle Eddie lived. He was a kind, laid-back guy and just let her do it.

One day Josephine slipped and fell down the stairs, and broke her pelvis. It was a miracle that she did not die right then and there. She was hospitalized for weeks, bound in a contraption that kept her body from moving while the bones healed.

With her release came new problems. She needed home assistance, and that person had to speak Polish, the only language she knew.

Stan put an ad in the Polish church newsletter, and within a week a woman by the name of Anne answered it. She said she was a divorced Polish immigrant and needed a job to support her children back in the home country. Stan thought she was the solution to all his problems, and at first it seemed he was right. Anne was well liked by both Stan and Josephine, and by other members of the family. My mother and father met Anne and enjoyed her company. My mother realized that if it were not for this woman, she herself would be pressed into being the caregiver. She was more than happy to let Anne fill that time-consuming role.

When I met Anne, I could psychically see unsettling things about her, but I kept my observations to myself. The family was happy with her and I did not want to be the cause of unpleasantness. I just let what I saw go, at least for the time being. I had to listen to family members talk about how great Anne was, and how she was a blessing. After a while, however, I could no longer stand the nonstop praising of this woman. I could see the real Anne, and I felt I had to finally speak my mind.

The opportunity came one Friday night when my family and I were returning from dinner in Jersey City. I sat through about ten minutes of flattery about Anne, and then I spoke up. "Don't trust her," I said. "She is a communist, thinks like a communist, and is plotting against the family."

My father was driving and was so startled that he almost had an accident. I expected him to swing around in his seat and rap me on the head with his fist. My mother and father verbally ripped into me. "How can you say that about her, she is a wonderful woman!"

Being psychic and seeing things that others cannot is not always a good thing. I endured the berating and said no more.

Josephine died in 1978. Her death devastated Stan, who was never the same. Not long after that, he suffered a stroke that left him incapacitated. Anne, already firmly embedded in the household, seamlessly switched gears from taking care of Josephine to taking care of Stan. From Stan's perspective, he replaced his over-indulging mother with another mother. Anne doted on him as if he were a little child, feeding him and wiping his mouth. It made family members cringe, no matter how much they liked Anne. Nonetheless, everyone was relieved he had someone to look after him.

Whenever I visited Uncle Stan, I looked into the eyes of Anne and could see more disturbing images. I felt she wanted to take over the house and get ahold of Stan's money. To keep peace, I kept quiet. It seemed things in the family were going well and I was not about to rock the boat. I could tell without benefit of any psychic ability that Anne knew I was wise to her, and did not like me.

Unlike other members of my family, I could not speak much Polish, though I could understand a good bit of it. Because of my limited Polish, I would speak to Stan in English, which she could not understand. She always assumed I was talking about her, and was suspicious of me.

As we all expected, Stan and Anne soon got married, and she moved into his apartment. Now the plot thickened. Everyone in the family, including Stan, thought she was the perfect wife. I thought the opposite, that Anne's trap was set and waiting for the right time to spring shut.

One of the first signs that my assessment of Anne was right was a change in her behavior. Soon, whenever I stopped by their apartment after dinnertime, I would find Anne getting herself dolled up, carefully putting on her makeup and fixing her hair. This was a sudden change, because in the past she had rarely worn makeup. I could psychically see a man that was on her mind—and it wasn't Stan. My conclusion: she had a boyfriend. Anne would tell Stan that she was going to see her cousins on Walnut Street. Stan was a trusting man and always told her, "Have a good time." Without a doubt, she most certainly did.

These "cousin visits" went from occasional to a daily routine. Uncle Eddie confided in me that he believed Anne had a boyfriend. I just smiled—that was old news to me.

Anne hated Uncle Eddie. He was an obstacle in her diabolical plot to acquire Stan's house and money. She tried everything to get rid of Uncle Eddie, calling him a sloppy housekeeper and unclean. She pestered Stan to throw him out. Stan resisted, but she kept the pressure on. What Anne did not understand was that Eddie and Stan, who were about the same age, grew up together. They went to the movies together, attended the same school and church, and even played on the same baseball team. They were not just relatives, but friends as well. Now that they were adults, they occasionally would get into verbal scraps, but those ties of youth always came through and bad feelings quickly dissipated. So, as long as Stan was around, Uncle Eddie was not going anywhere.

Eventually the situation changed. Uncle Eddie had many medical issues that worsened. He was admitted into Columbus Hospital, where his daughter, Diana, worked in the administration department. I visited him often at the hospital and I always found him in good spirits. It came as a shock when I heard that he died.

It looked like Anne's wish was coming true. Eddie was gone and the complete takeover of Stan's property and money was nearly in hand. To make sure the property continued to bring in rental income, Anne wanted a Polish family to move into Eddie's first-floor apartment right away. They had to be Polish so she could understand everything they said. My family now saw Anne turn from an angelic woman helping Stan to an evil woman from hell. Two days after Eddie's funeral, she marched prospective Polish renters through the apartment while Diana and I were trying to remove his belongings. It seemed quite disrespectful.

I stood close to Anne during the cleanup and received disturbing psychic images from her. To put it bluntly, Anne wanted to murder Stan. I could see it was a plot concocted by Anne and her boyfriend. Alarmed, I could not remain silent. I warned every member of the family I could reach. "Anne will try to kill Uncle Stan,"

I told them. "If he dies in some mysterious or odd way, I will contact the police to investigate his death." I ended my calls by saying, "Now you know, so when it happens, don't say you're surprised."

Sadly, my family thought I was nuts, but to me it did not matter. From a moral perspective, they were properly warned. I knew that it was only a matter of time before Anne sprang that trap of hers.

Anne and Stan had a shopping routine. Anne would do the shopping and bring the bags of groceries through the front door and up the stairs, and place them on the second floor landing. Stan would take the bags from the landing to the kitchen table. On one particular shopping day, Anne hatched her plot. She placed a bag of groceries on the landing, and when Stan grabbed the bag, she did not let go, but pulled the bag downward. She stood back against the railing, giving Stan a clear path to fall down the stairs.

It worked. Stan lost his balance and tumbled down the stairs. Anne looked at his body lying at the foot of the stairs, but to her horror, Stan started moving—he was not dead! Like his mother who had fallen down those same stairs years before and lived, so did Stan.

The world changed for Anne overnight. When I heard the news of the fall, I rushed to the hospital. I found Anne sitting in a chair about ten feet from Stan's bed. Psychic images poured out of her like a high definition television program. I could see her pulling on the grocery bag and getting out of the way of his fall, and especially felt her thoughts of how she was going to explain this botched murder attempt and make it seem like a horrible accident.

With Stan's survival, Anne's boyfriend left her high and dry. I was certain he wanted no part of this disaster. The days of Anne getting dolled up were over. With her lover on the run, she resumed looking like a peasant farm worker. The worse part for her was yet to come, for now she had to take care of her husband, who was in even worse physical condition than when he had his stroke. In addition, her golden relationship with other family members began to tarnish. Perhaps they now suspected her as I did.

The fall left its mark on Stan. He became forgetful, and at times would be downright nasty to Anne. Her whole plan backfired, and her life became a living hell. Months passed and things continued to get worse. Stan needed her around the clock, and she was a prisoner of that five-room apartment. Now whenever I stopped by, she looked at me with fear and began shaking. She was aware that I knew exactly what happened. She was fearful that I would expose her. She could not wait for me to leave.

Stan's health quickly declined, and finally he had to be taken to the hospital. Even during those last days, there was no reprieve for Anne. She sat with him day after day with nothing to read or anyone to talk to. The hospital's staff spoke only English, Spanish, and Portuguese, no Polish.

One night when she returned home from the hospital, she went into Stan's desk and grabbed all his legal papers, tearing up whatever she could get her hands on. I was certain she was told by someone that if there was no last will and testament, everything Stan had would go to her.

By this point, Stan's mind was just about gone. He could not even recognize family members who came to visit him. If any one of us asked him about his last will and testament, he did know what we were talking about. The family did not know who was his lawyer. Stan had always been very secretive, and that worked in Anne's favor. At least that part of her plan worked. Early one morning at the hospital, Stan died, and Anne prepared to inherit everything.

About six months after the funeral, all the paperwork for the estate was settled. Anne sold everything and went back to Poland. My guess is that with the property value of the house and his savings, she went back with more than half a million dollars.

My initial and later psychic impressions about Anne and her motives were correct. I was able to see her real personality and have a full understanding of what she was plotting. If Stan had died from the fall, I would have pursued my promise to have the police investigate his death as murder. Since he survived the fall, it would have been impossible to prove attempted murder based on my psychic visions.

Karma got Anne in the end. Despite getting a great deal of money, she left the United States a bitter woman. Years had passed, and she was returning to Poland an old woman. We heard from a family member that her family back home did not like her, and that she had become a bitter and mean person, especially to her children from her first marriage and their families.

In the end, Anne's plotting, deceit, and manipulations to get Stan's wealth was successful—but it took too many years to get it, and at a big price. The man she really wanted ran when the going got tough, leaving her to fend for herself. Even my family, who were once her biggest supporters, turned on her in the end.

But her biggest fear was not my mother or the other family members—it was me, the psychic nephew of her husband. I am convinced that she felt I could read her mind. Without saying a word, my presence made her uncomfortable from the beginning to the very end.

Did she think it was all worth it? She did not have much time to enjoy her spoils. Anne died a mere six years after Stan.

My mother and brother finally admitted that what I told them about Anne was accurate. To this very day when the subject of Anne and Stan comes up at family gatherings, my mother will say, "You were right about her all along."

11

Ingo Swann

One of the most remarkable men I ever met was Ingo Swann, an unusual psychic who had an influence on my ability and career. Ingo, who died in 2013, was an enigma to most people, even those who claimed to have known him well. If you have not heard his name, you have probably heard of the term "remote viewing," which is a form of clairvoyance that involves being able to locate and see a distant site by using geographic coordinates.

Ingo was a major force in the development of "controlled remote viewing" at the Stanford Research Institute in California, where he worked with Russell Targ and Harold Putoff. His positive results in experiments caught the attention of the Central Intelligence Agency, who later funded The Stargate Project, which some refer to as the United States' involvement in psychic spying. Stargate was "officially" ended in 1995, but went underground into the black budget.

Ingo evidently was born with remarkable psychic abilities. He was born in 1933 in Telluride, Colorado. His father was a truck driver. He had his first out-of-body experience at age three when he had his tonsils out. At the same time, he began to see auras around all living things. By age nine, he projected himself out to the Milky Way. Later in life, he said he visited Jupiter and saw its unknown rings, long before NASA's Voyager probe arrived there and documented them. Ingo also remotely viewed the dark side of the moon, and said aliens had bases there.

As you can imagine, Ingo was a complex person. Aside from being a remote viewer, he was also an artist and author. His oil paintings reflected what he saw and experienced while remote viewing and traveling out-of-body through the cosmos. He had, at least for much of his life, tremendous psychic abilities. I never knew Ingo to refer to himself as a psychic, however, but he would show these abilities to me often.

If you ask twenty-five people who knew Ingo Swann what he was like, each would give a different description of the man they knew. This is my personal account of the man.

We first met in 1998 at his building in the Bowery, a street name and also a section of Manhattan. Ingo had sent word to my friend Paula Roberts that he wanted to meet me. He told Paula that he had heard about a psychic named Karl from people who frequented the Parapsychology Foundation.

I was at the foundation when Paula approached me with his invitation, and I was intrigued. Within a few days, Paula and I were at Ingo's doorstep, a brownstone of which he was part owner. The Bowery is a sketchy part of the city, and as I got to know Ingo better, I saw how it suited him. Ingo liked living on the edge.

We were told to enter his building and take the stairs to the basement. At the base of the stairs was a huge room that was dimly lit. This, I learned, was where he spent most of his time. It was both his studio and office. There was a large table near the stairs that was surrounded by his enormous original paintings; some were at least eight feet wide and six feet high. I would describe his art as interstellar, with images of far-off planets and galaxies.

Suspended above the table was the light source, an electric cord with a single forty-watt light bulb hanging from it. Above the bulb was a home-made shade made from a piece of crinkled aluminum foil. The light revealed the lower half of a nose, beard and mouth biting down on a two-and-a-half-inch cigar that glowed red, followed by a blue puff of smoke. The man behind the blue smoke was Ingo Swann.

Ingo Swann and psychic Noreen Renier

He motioned to chairs across from him and said, "Sit down, relax." We sat, but did not relax.

Now, up close, I could see his eyes. I felt he could see through me, and it made me feel uneasy. Paula, who had known Ingo for years, began the conversation by introducing me and told him how we first met. He kept staring at me and occasionally glanced at Paula. I started feeling pressure in the front of my head and a slight ringing in my ears. I knew what this meant—it was a common happening for me. I was about to experience *imprints*, or images from the past, that existed in this basement.

I turned my head and next to the stairs I had a vision of a man standing at a workbench wearing an apron, and another man walking around the room. Ingo interrupted Paula and asked me what was I seeing.

I answered, "Imprints. There is a man by the stairs at a workbench and another man walking around the floor."

Paula looked at us both, waiting to hear what Ingo had to say about this.

He answered, "I see them, too. I believe the man's name is Frankie."

I was astonished. For the first time in my life, someone could see what I was seeing and it made me feel wonderful.

Then Ingo said, "This was once a factory. They had workers and machinery down here."

I could tell Ingo was impressed by my ability to see these imprints. I had made an excellent impression on him, which pleased me greatly.

My uneasiness of being with Ingo disappeared by the end of the day. When I left I knew we had become friends because he said to me, "Stop by any time. Just call so I know you're coming." I soon learned that Ingo rarely gave such invitations.

From time to time I would phone him for help with a problem, and on a few occasions I would stop by. Every time I showed up at his door, I made sure that I had a bag of cigars. The cigars were in self-defense. The stubby cigars Ingo smoked were God-awful and drove me crazy, so one day I decided to bring him something of quality to smoke.

There was a Cuban immigrant who had a small cigar shop at his home in Newark. "Dave The Cuban," as he was known in the neighborhood, would make hand-rolled cigars on a wooden bench in his kitchen. Dave asked me what kind of guy I was buying his cigars for. No way was I going to explain the real Ingo, so I just said, "A guy who smokes awful cigars and spends most of his time in the basement painting pictures."

Dave said, "For this man, buy him a bag of 'blems.'"

Blems, (short for blemished) are cigars that Dave rejected because they did not come out perfect, and were half the price of his perfect cigars.

Ingo loved the blems. So, anytime I stopped by, I treated Ingo to his new favorite cigars. Ironically, I still never saw him smoke a cigar that was more than three inches, even though the blems were longer. Maybe he cut them to a smaller size when I wasn't looking? Nothing surprised me about Ingo.

Ingo became my "go to" guy when I had a problem that concerned my psychic ability. One day I was looking in a magazine and I saw a serving tray with the image of a pack of Lucky Strike cigarettes as they were packaged in the 1940s. Back then the cigarettes came in a soft dark green pack. Something about those cigarettes bothered me all day. I could not get the image out of my head. I lost sleep that night for many hours. The cigarettes then kept me awake for entire nights on end. I went to see Ingo because I thought he might help me figure out what my problem was.

We sat at the large table with that forty-watt bulb hanging over our heads, and then Ingo walked over to his desk and brought a stack of photocopy paper to the table. He handed me a pencil and a sheet of paper. "Draw what you see," he said.

I began to draw the cigarette pack. As I was nearing the end of the drawing, Ingo pulled the paper away from me and threw it on the floor. He handed me another sheet and said, "Draw it again."

This routine went on and on, until the floor was littered with my half-drawn sketches. Each time I began to draw, he would ask me what I was seeing. Then, with each drawing, I began to expand my vision from the cigarette pack to things around it. "Soldiers, I see American soldiers," I said. Again the paper was taken from me and joined the others on the floor. It didn't take long before the story expanded more and I saw soldiers taking cases of cigarettes off landing crafts and onto a beach.

I asked Ingo why this happened to me. He just stared back at me without an answer. I was left to figure out the meaning of it on my own. That night, the images of green-packed *Lucky Strikes* were gone, and I finally had a decent night's sleep. Ingo never gave me an explanation for what I experienced. This was typical behavior on his part. He would toy with people from time to time. Just like the little kid who says, "I know something you don't know."

About a year later I stumbled upon a possible answer to this Lucky Strike riddle. I recalled that when I visited my father, who was living in Georgia. I asked him about some of the things he was involved with during World War II. He spoke of unloading LSTs with supplies after the troops landed on the Kwajalein Atoll in the Marshall Islands (the Battle of Kwajalein was fought from January 31-February 3, 1944). An LST was a landing ship tank that supported amphibious operations, and carried troops, equipment, and supplies to land.

My father said, "We unloaded ammunition, weapons, food, coffee, and cigarettes." I was convinced that memories from my father were passed onto me. I have no other explanation. For me the story was now complete to my satisfaction.

There were always people stopping by to see Ingo. He rarely introduced me to these visitors when they came by while I was there. Some were dressed in work clothes and others in suits. He usually told them to stop by later. I still wonder who these people were.

Sometimes Ingo would test my abilities, and other times he would ask me for help. He once confided in me about an odd situation he was having and thought I could help him out with it. His building was a four-story brick structure, and he rented out space as loft apartments. For some reason, he could not keep one of the lofts rented. People would move in, and soon would move out. He asked me to check out the loft and tell him what I saw or felt.

As I walked through the loft, I could see that at one time, many years ago, the entire floor was used for storage. I saw stacks of wooden crates reaching from the floor and to almost the top of the twelve-foot-high ceilings. I also saw a small room with a toilet located in one corner of the floor. While looking at this corner, I felt that a man had died in that room. I turned to the staircase to see images of policemen dressed in turn-of-the-century uniforms coming up the stairs. Neighbors, mostly women and children, clogged the stairway as the policemen struggled their way up. Could it be that the spirit of this deceased man from the room with the toilet was hanging around spooking the tenants?

I returned to the basement where Ingo was waiting for me. He had original blueprints of the building from the late 1800s, showing that the floor was marked "storage" and there was a toilet located in the corner, exactly where I had seen it. I had been asked to check out the room and not to make conclusions as to why the tenants always moved out. My job was finished, but I was certain that Ingo spoke to Paula Roberts, who was there at the time, about a way to remove this troubled spirit.

Ingo was the most unique person I ever met. Each meeting with him was an event. I don't believe anyone knew the full extent of his psychic abilities. I am convinced he made it a point to shield his true powers because it would scare those around him.

Once I was invited to a party he gave for Paula's mother, who was visiting from England. He disliked people who showed up late, so everyone did their best to be on time. On this day I was traveling through the Holland Tunnel, which connects New Jersey with New York. There was an accident that caused a major traffic jam and I was stuck in the tunnel. I kept looking at my watch and soon I was late for the party. I looked toward the floor of the passenger seat and suddenly saw Ingo's face superimposed on it. His image said, "You're late."

I got angry and started yelling, "I'm stuck in the tunnel and there is nothing I can do, I'll get there as soon as I can!"

Finally, I got through the traffic and made my way to the party. Once in the room, I saw Ingo with his back to me holding a drink in his hand talking to one of the guests. As I was approaching him, he spun around, and before I could say a word, he said, "You didn't have to yell at me."

Had he been remote viewing me? No, more likely, he had remotely projected himself. What else could this man do? Most of us will never know.

Toward the end of his life, Ingo wanted to be left alone. His friends tried to visit but he would not have it. He would get angry and snap at them. For months, I wanted to visit, but I decided not to ask, and instead waited hopefully for him to get better before I called on him.

Perhaps he was not feeling well, or thought he no longer looked his best. He had lost some of his teeth. I recalled that once, after leaving a video rental store, Ingo and I stopped to rest at a local park. He told me that he had searched my name at the video store and saw all the films I produced that were available there for rent. He was impressed.

This was a perfect opportunity for me to get his permission to make a documentary of his life. I tried to make my case for the project: there was plenty of available footage, his friends would be happy to help with it, and he would be there to make sure it was right. When I finally finished my proposal, he took a puff on his cigar, looked at me, and said, "No. Where were you twenty years ago when I was good-looking?"

Maybe the thought of people seeing him at his worst was something he could not bear.

Sadly, the chance to visit did not come, and I never spoke to him again. He died on January 31, 2013.

Ingo's sister held a memorial service at his favorite museum. I arrived there with Dr. McMahon and her husband, Tom. We were the first to arrive. Tom and I helped set up the chairs, which extended into two rooms. They expected a full house. When all the people arrived there was standing room only. A handful of people made speeches and reminisced about their connection with Ingo. The service ended with an impressive slide show of Ingo through the years. After the service, everyone was invited to a local restaurant and treated to drinks and hors d'oeuvres. At the end of the night, we all went our separate ways.

I was hoping Ingo would speak to me from beyond, but as of this writing, he has not. I have not given up hope, because I believe he will—it is just a matter of time. What I learned from our friendship is that you cannot rush Ingo.

Rest in peace Ingo Swann.

12

The Forgotten Dead

I once asked Ingo Swann if was there anything that he regretted seeing while he was remote viewing. The question brought a painful look to his face. He hesitated for a moment, then turned to me and said, "Once, when I saw the place where people were tortured." I immediately dropped that line of questioning. I could only imagine the horror and pain he must have witnessed.

Not long after that, I was witness to another kind of horror and pain: the unending anguish over the death of loved ones, intensified by the careless treatment given the poor. The horror and sadness are impossible to erase from the mind. I have not been spared those unpleasant mental voyages.

One day, I received a call from my good friend, Anna, who is a lawyer. She asked me to take some pictures and video footage of a piece of property in Newark, located directly across from Newark (Liberty) Airport. She needed the material for a litigation case. I agreed, and the following day we met at my house and drove out to the property.

When we arrived, and before I could turn the engine off, I felt an uneasy feeling in the pit of my stomach. The first thing I noticed was the stillness in the air. Although we were in an area next to the airport and adjacent to a major highway where the noise is deafening at times, the place seemed very quiet and still—perhaps too quiet and still. If I had taken a moment to think, I might have remembered that out-of-place quiet and stillness usually comes right before I have a vision.

I moved to the back of my truck, took out my tripod, and started setting up my video camera with a freshly charged battery and a digital tape. I slung my 35-mm still camera around my neck, closed the tailgate, and walked toward the property. As I was crossing the ground, I felt uneasiness radiating beneath my feet, similar to the way someone might feel if they were walking on top of a freshly manicured lawn after reading a sign, "Keep off the Grass." But this ground was no manicured lawn. It was filled with broken glass, rocks, pieces of wood, countless fast food wrappers and containers, discarded concrete barriers from the roadway, and piles of asphalt and dirt.

I panned the video from east to west. From the corner of my eye, I noticed Anna standing very quietly at the northern end of the property. I moved my video camera to the railroad tracks at the west end of the property, lining it up to take a north/south pan. Anna walked across my field of vision, moved to an area I had already videotaped, and kept herself out of camera range. In between the video shoots, I used my still camera to take random shots of the piles of garbage.

Around the perimeter were large patches of yellow field grass, some reaching as high as two feet. A slight breeze bent the grass, making it look like the western prairie. Yet, when I looked closely, I saw that the grass shielded unsightly trash beneath it.

The uneasy feeling in the pit of my stomach stayed with me, but I could not let that distract me. This was a legal case, and there was a lot riding on the images that I could capture with my camera.

When I was called on an assignment like this, I always focused all my attention on the job at hand, making sure that everything went right.

The pauper's cemetery, now overgrown with weeds

Despite my concentration, I could not ignore the images that were forming in my mind. They were pictures of the past: a horse-drawn wagon stacked with crudely built rectangle boxes that was moving slowly down the road leading into this area; men, covered with dirt and sweat, and carrying shovels, who were gathered in small groups around the property; and men, women, and children who were standing next to some of those boxes, crying.

"Anna, what's this place all about?" I asked.

She answered, "This was a pauper's graveyard."

Once Anna said, "pauper's graveyard," it all made sense to me and left me with a sickening feeling.

From the mid-1800s to 1954, indigent people who died were buried in this cemetery by families that could not afford to bury them in one of the many prestigious cemeteries that were scattered throughout Newark area. Newark was full of these poor, who were unrecognized in life and unwanted in death.

From the mid- to late nineteenth century, Newark was a booming industrial city, with tanneries, manufacturing plants, stores, and schools. The job opportunities lured tens of thousands of immigrants who poured out of Ellis Island and onto the streets of New York City and New Jersey's larger cities, including Newark and nearby Jersey City. Most of them arrived with little more than the clothes on their backs. They lived in wretched conditions in quickly-built tenement housing, and often made barely enough money to survive. There was no money left over for the costs of death. My own family was a good example, as I described earlier— my grandparents immigrated from Poland and Russia, leaving behind farms for factories.

But don't be fooled that having housing and a job made everything work out well for these immigrants, and that it was smooth sailing from then on. Quite the opposite was true. Most had grown up on farms and knew nothing about working in a factory. The long hours and low pay for doing a monotonous, repetitive job took its toll on the workers and their families. Taverns operated on almost every corner, because drinking seemed to make working these dead-end jobs more bearable.

Drinking created drunks, and drunks made misery for their families. Sadly, after doing his share in producing a handful of children, my grandfather abandoned them shortly after his wife, my grandmother, died giving birth to my mother. Luckily for my mother, her aunt—her mother's sister, Josephine—offered to raise her. The other children were sent to an orphanage in Lodi, a town about ten miles from Newark. My grandfather was a heavy drinker and, in all probability, died penniless, and could very well be one of the unfortunate anonymous ones buried at this very site.

I thought about all this as I finished and packed away my camera gear. Anna and I left the cemetery about mid-afternoon. I may have left the grounds, but the psychic images of that site reappeared to me that night as I tried to sleep. Again I witnessed images that were bizarre to me because they were a century old: foremen yelling to the diggers, wagon drivers calling out to ask for help unloading the bodies, men cursing, and horses snorting. The families watched the boxes, some large and some very small, filled with the remains of their loved ones, slide down the dirt piles and into a freshly dug trench—a mass grave. The men standing in the trench positioned the boxes side by side to maximize the number of occupants they could fit into it. The crying mourners got in the way of the workers. I heard Italian and a number of Eastern European languages as workers called out to the bereaved to step aside to let the men do their work. To see those boxes, large and small, being placed in the ground on this one given day, compounded my feelings of sadness. At one point, I saw a woman throw herself into the trench and wrap her arms around a coffin box. A worker dropped his shovel and he, shedding tears himself, pleaded with the woman to leave the cemetery and go home.

The faces and voices of people long gone still linger in a dimension that only someone like me can see. Today, the dirt road that brought the wagons to the cemetery has disappeared. The wooden shed at the north side of the property, where shovels, horse feed, buckets, and lanterns were kept, has faded into oblivion. I was an absent witness to one particular day, taken out of one hundred years of burials.

I had to keep in mind that I was hired to take the pictures and video for litigation, not to make psychic observations. Frankly, few really care about what happened so many years ago, or that this huge plot of ground held the remains of so many emotionally devastated families at a time when the city's growth was in high gear.

The litigation Anna was involved in dealt with the city's neglect of this cemetery and how it affected a woman whose father's grave had been turned into a garbage dump. At some point in the past, all signs, grave markers, and anything else indicating that this had ever been a cemetery had been removed, and the city of Newark began leasing out parts of the cemetery to various businesses. In the 1960s, part of the land was turned into an industrial storage yard. As a bonus, the city now had a place to dump tons of roadside debris and garbage.

What the city *didn't* count on was a man named George Spade, who was buried here in 1921, or his daughter, who, after all these years, was still alive and wanted to have her father disinterred and buried in the family plot in Hackensack. That started the whole legal case against the city of Newark and quickly became a featured story in the local newspapers. Unfortunately for George Spade's daughter, there was no way to locate the body of her father, now resting in a mass grave under dirt, debris, and a coating of asphalt. The scant records that may have been kept in those days concerning people who had no money or influence had been conveniently lost in a flood in the basement of the city's Hall of Records. Not to mention the likelihood that Spade's remains, buried unpreserved in a wooden box, had probably long since dissolved into the earth.

The city claimed that about 18,000 graves were at the site, while others put that number at an astounding 200,000! The second and higher estimate is probably accurate. According to existing records, among the dead buried beneath this garbage dump are veterans of the Revolutionary War, Civil War, Spanish American War, World War I, World War II, and Korean War (some of these older graves dating to the 1700s had been reinterred here from older Newark cemeteries); Native Americans; former slaves; immigrants from all over the world; and the thousands upon thousands of poor people from Newark and the surrounding area. In 1918 alone, 2,200 people died from the Spanish influenza epidemic in the city of Newark—and many of them probably wound up here in mass graves.

Yet with orders from City Hall and a few strokes of a pen, all signs that these hundreds of thousands of people had once existed had been erased.

I returned to the cemetery with my friend and confidant, psychic Paula Roberts, to get her impression of this site. Paula walked the site with an air of reverence. She treated this dumping ground/pauper's cemetery with respect, no differently than if she were walking on the grounds of the beautiful Arlington National Cemetery in Virginia. She looked up at me and said she "felt" many children buried here. Her face showed great sadness, knowing the circumstances behind these burials.

"Thousands upon thousands are here," she said.

I stood in the knee-high grass looking at Paula, who kept staring at the landscape and listening, as if voices were calling out to her. Paula was wearing a white dress and sweater, and as the sun was going down, her back shielded the sun, making the sun's rays beam around her, giving her a saint-like image.

It was getting late. We stood together to give the site a final look, and, without saying a word, we boarded my truck and left.

My experiences prompted me to research the property, and I found some remarkable facts about it. Back in the late 1700s, the site was known as the Bond House. From November 22-28, 1776, General George Washington made the Bond House his headquarters. The small cottages on the land were used as an encampment for members of Washington's staff.

Later, around 1878, the city relocated thousands of burials here: 500 to 700 graves from a local Newark almshouse (a poor house), and 4,500 graves from the city's public cemetery, then located on Ann Street and Hamburg Place, now re-named Wilson Avenue. In 1888, the city tore down the Bond House and erected a new caretaker building. That building is no longer standing.

Now, in the twenty-first century, there is no one alive who can remember the dirt road leading into the cemetery or the wooden shed facing the north side that stored the shovels, horse feed, and lanterns. The sights and sounds of horse-drawn wagons, the mourners, and workers are all gone from the memories of the living, except for mine, because those images I *still* see, the voices spoken at the site I *can still hear,* clearly. Those sights and sounds will remain with me for as long as I am alive.

When I decided to write about this, I returned to the cemetery to take photos of its present condition to include in this book. About ten years had passed since the litigation case. As a result of the case, the city of Newark built a memorial on the site. A plaque on a stone marker explains that this was once a cemetery and is hallowed ground. The city also landscaped the area and added park benches.

Locked cemetery gates

When I arrived, I was shocked to see that a cyclone fence had been installed around the property. The gate was padlocked, so that access to the public was denied, not only to the entire cemetery, but to the stone marker! I asked myself, *why did the city of Newark even bother to build this memorial?* It was one more insult to the dead.

Close to my house is the huge Holy Cross Cemetery in North Arlington. The cemetery stretches seven-tenths of a mile on the Schuyler Avenue side. A hundred years from now, will it be acceptable for us to remove the headstones and markers and build condominiums on this land, so that wealthy tenants can have a great view of New York City? Those condos would be resting on thousands of forgotten graves. Do the future generations have the right to determine the worth of a cemetery versus the dollar value of its land? Let's hope that our humanity does not descend to this kind of thinking.

Seeing the poor, grieving faces of people long gone still makes a strong impression on me. Born with an ability to visit a world that existed long before my own, I am, once again, the *Absent Witness*.

13

A Visit with the Dead

Over the years, whenever I am in northeast Pennsylvania, I often stop by St. Mary's Cemetery in Plymouth, to visit the graves of some of my family members, which include my grandfather, Alexander, and various aunts, uncles, and a few cousins. I find St. Mary's Cemetery a strange place. The moment I drive onto its grounds, I feel I enter an insubstantial zone. The sound and feel of the place is "different." It is hard to put into words. The air seems unnaturally still and sounds do not seem to carry much further than a few feet in front of your face. The atmosphere is similar to what I experienced at the paupers' gravesite in Newark.

What's more, St. Mary's is not easy to find—many maps do not show it, and its entrance is off a side street, marked by a small sign with an arrow. If Hollywood had to construct a quick cemetery for a film, it would look like St. Mary's, a field of gravestones with a simple road that loops through it.

During my visits, I make it a point to stay a little longer at my grandfather's grave. It has his name, Alexander Pietrzykowski, and the date of his death, December 7, 1945. I never knew my grandfather Alexander because he died years before I was born. The only information I have about him has been from stories told by my father and his brothers and sisters. Yet, when I visit his grave, I feel as if he knows that I'm there and he wants to meet me.

Karl Petry at the Gravestone of Alexander Pietrzykowski

The first time this happened, I brushed it off as just something I was wishing for. The next time I visited, a few years later, it happened again. This time I didn't dismiss it and went along with the psychic feelings and images.

After this particular visit, I drove home to New Jersey, which is a little over a two-hour drive. A series of images went through my mind all the way home. I could see town streets, and people's faces;

I was able to recognize a few of the streets as being from the town of Plymouth. Alexander actually lived in the town of Larksville, which is a small town next to Plymouth, which had a busy Main Street filled with bars, stores, and the Shawnee Theater. The showing of cowboy movies was so prevalent that the locals called the theater "the shootin' gallery."

That night I tossed and turned for hours. Images kept getting stronger, and no matter how hard I tried to get rid of those images, the more they appeared and the stronger they got. It must have been well into the morning hours when I experienced calmness. The multitude of images were gone, and in its place I felt myself walking down Shawnee Avenue in Plymouth. Judging by the few cars parked on the street, the year must have been in the mid- to late 1930s. I walked down the street until I came upon a white house with a metal fence to my right. On the porch, a woman was putting clothes on a clothesline: a few white things and a handful of men's work clothes. No doubt her husband was a miner just like Alexander. She smiled at me and nodded her head to enter the house. Inside I saw Alexander and three other men sitting at the kitchen table. In front of each one was a glass. A bottle of *Four Roses* whiskey sat in the center of the table.

Alexander pointed to an empty chair beside him and told me to sit. He then introduced me to the other men in the room. Each had a Slavic-sounding name. Alexander, speaking with a thick Polish accent, told me what it was like to be a miner, and the hard work they did. Each of the men would join in and boast about how strong they were, and how loading the tons of coal meant nothing to them. Within minutes a glass was put in front of me. I resisted the whiskey and just sat back listening to these men go on and on with their stories. Alexander made it a point to single me out and go into details about his life, all the time smiling at me as if he had finally met up with his long-lost relative.

My visit felt like it lasted for hours. I can still recall this event in such detail and clarity as if it happened an hour ago. As the conversation slowed down, I could tell Alexander was getting tired and the other men at the table were nodding off, so it was time for me to leave. I stood up and extended my hand to Alexander. He stood up and stared into my eyes and hugged me. I could not find any words to say to him, I just put on a smile, turned and left. I walked down the stairs of the house and headed toward the black and silver metal gate, but had the urge to turn around. The clothesline woman stood on the porch looking at me with a look of wonder, or, some would say, a questionable look. That scared me. It was then I realized that *I* was a ghost. I had entered their time and place, yet I did not exist in it. Alexander, his buddies, and the woman were real and I was a visitor or intruder.

Parapsychology and afterlife studies literature document many cases in which the dead appear to the living as though they were still alive. Typically, these cases occur soon after a person has died (and sometimes the living do not know that death has taken place). Conversations and even physical contact take place. The visits often end with a fading away of the dead person, or an abrupt disappearance.

The reverse may happen as well, and I believe that this is what happened to me. I was a living person visiting the world of the dead, which, of course, is real to them. I arrived at the house in a curious state, looking and acting like a mortal, but by the time I left and headed for the fence, I had become something else. I might have started to look transparent, the way we would see a ghost. I also realized that I didn't belong there, and that reinforced my status as a ghost. The look from the woman confirmed this.

Now you can see how this incident has formed my opinion and attitude regarding ghosts. If there is a way to communicate with them—if they have something to share with us—let them in their own way, either through thoughts, dreams, or actual appearance, present themselves to us. Let us not behave badly, swinging infrared cameras into their faces, and yelling at them to "do something" to prove they are there. I would hate to think that a modern day bunch of "ghost hunters" were trying to entertain themselves by doing these annoying things to Alexander and his friends or to any ghosts they encounter.

Other cultures treat their deceased with respect. I have a good friend who is Chinese named Qi, who has built a memorial altar in her home for her departed mother. It has her mother's picture along with personal items placed around it. Her culture gives respect to the dead and there is no talk to disturb their spirits with *hunting* them down like some kind of sport. This same practice can be found in other Asian cultures, and elsewhere around the world.

I realize that my views may not be popular with hard core "ghost hunters," but I am firmly convinced that they resonate with many others who have looked for ways to stay connected to their departed loved ones. When I get involved with situations regarding spirits, I treat the situation with the utmost reverence. I will do my best to continue down this path.

Testimonials

Karen McLean
High school teacher

As a thirty-eight-year veteran of teaching public high school English, I am always on the look-out for ways to make my teaching more exciting, both for my students and myself. Since 2010, Karl Petry has been the "big draw" for the students who wind up with me as their English teacher and for the students who choose take my elective course "Supernatural Literature." Each year, Karl donates an entire day of his time—free of charge—to mesmerize eighty to one hundred students by telling them about his many investigations of hauntings and other supernatural phenomena, and he always leaves my students with an experience they'll never forget.

One year, Karl was questioned by a teacher in the audience about demons—not one of Karl's favorite subjects—who admitted that he had many tattoos of symbols meant to ward off attacks by demons. Karl assured the teacher that the presence of the tattoos could, indeed, help ward off demons, and as he spoke, he gestured with his index fingers to the entire length of the insides of both his own arms. The teacher became quite shaken, and asked Karl, "Why did you just point to your arms that way?"

Karl replied, "Because that's where you have your tattoos."

At once, the teacher rolled up both sleeves of his shirt and revealed to the audience both arms, tattooed from shoulder to wrist, but on the insides of the arms, as opposed to the typical outside location. As the students and others in the audience shivered, the teacher asked Karl, "May I shake your hand?" and then promptly left, clearly shaken.

On another occasion, as Karl was speaking to my students, he stopped his presentation to address a female student who was seated in the front row. This young lady had often seemed to me to be very sad and awkward around her peers.

"I'm sorry," he said, "but your thoughts are colliding with my thoughts and making it very difficult for me to concentrate. He then explained to her that she is an "empath," one who can actually feel the emotions of the people around her. For instance, he told her, if someone sitting near you feels depressed, you will feel depressed, as well, even though it isn't your depression you're feeling!"

The relief on the young woman's face was indescribable, but her smile said it all. She and Karl spoke after his presentation, and I believe they keep in touch today. He clearly helped her understand what had been going on in her own mind—perhaps her whole life— and gave her great hope and reassurance that she wasn't "crazy," which is something most people who think they may have psychic powers fear the most.

One year, after he was finished with his presentation, the line of students waiting to speak privately to Karl wound around the room. Finally, it was turn for one of the students from my Creative Writing class. This young lady had spent most of the year writing very sad poetry about a male friend of hers who had lost his life in a car accident the previous summer, so it was no surprise to me when she handed Karl a photograph of the young man, and asked him if he could tell her anything about the boy in the photo. Karl instantly knew that the boy was deceased, but then something strange happened. The deceased young man began speaking "through" Karl and he relayed the words of the deceased to the girl. He spoke of the sports team jersey he had been buried in and many other details of not only his funeral but of his life. At one point, Karl told the girl, "Wait a minute. He's talking so fast I can't keep up with him."

Karl continued to speak the boy's thoughts to the shocked student. And finally, Karl said, through the boy's voice, "You have my sneakers."

The girl broke down crying, and told everyone that she did, indeed, have the deceased's sneakers in the back of her bedroom closet.

At Karl's 2015 presentation, he had been specifically asked by a teacher, who directs many school plays, to go upstairs above the auditorium, into the control booth. Apparently this teacher and others had frequently seen, from the stage or from the floor of the auditorium, "someone" pacing back and forth in the control booth while the lights were off and when no one was supposed to be up there. Also, the lights in the auditorium would sometimes turn off in the middle of a rehearsal—when no one was standing anywhere near the light switch, which was on the back wall in clear view of everyone.

Karl and I both went up into the control booth, ascending more of a ladder than a staircase, and Karl told me that he could feel the presence of a spirit—or spirits—that had been there at some point, but that none were there now. Then he looked out of the window of the control booth, down into the auditorium, and pointed down there and said to me, "But there's someone—a spirit—down there right now. I have to go down."

Down we went, but I decided to stay outside to allow Karl the time and solitude he might need to deal with whomever—or whatever—had beckoned to him. When I returned, I brought with me the teacher who had asked us to go up into the control room. Karl told us that the spirit had been talking about the play *Oklahoma!* and how a certain line from the song should be sung. The teacher with us began to cry, telling us that *Oklahoma!*

had been the favorite Broadway show of one of her best friends, a teacher at our school, who had been deceased for some years. Karl then described his physical appearance exactly as it had been, imitated his voice, his walk and his hand gestures. Another teacher brought in a photograph of the teacher, and Karl smiled and said, "That's our boy!"

As shaken as we all were, we felt peaceful knowing that our former friend and colleague was still "hanging around" with us.

As far as my own "psychic" experiences with Karl go, I have only a few, because I have always felt that I didn't want to "use" my friend for his "powers." Once, however, I really needed his help.

I had been out with my daughter, touring a college campus, when I received a very urgent call on my cell phone. The caller gave me the phone number of a doctor who I needed to see as soon as possible. We were having lunch at the time, and I scribbled the phone number down—somewhere. Of course, the next day, I couldn't find the number anywhere and feared that I had written it down on a napkin which had probably ended up in the trash at the college. I emailed Karl right away and explained my dilemma.

Almost instantly, he emailed me back "Do you keep a small, red notebook in your purse?" he asked.

I instantly knew where to look. In my purse I had two checkbooks, one in a blue cover and one in a red cover. I opened the one with the red cover, and there was the phone number, written right across the top of the first page of the check registry! I could not have been more grateful to my friend!

On another occasion, I had misplaced my car keys and had been driving with my spares for more than a week. I had been resisting the urge to ask Karl—again, I did not want to "use" my friend for such things—but I was desperate. I began my email with an apology—I just hated asking him for things I thought he might think trivial, but he graciously answered me with his usual kindness.

"They're inside a big, white, fluffy purse," he said.

"I don't own a big, white, fluffy purse," I answered.

I thought that was that. If Karl couldn't "see" my keys, they must truly be gone. A couple of days later, I was sorting out winter coats, deciding which ones to take up to the attic. In the back of the pile was a coat I usually wore only when I went out to shovel snow—a big, white, fluffy coat with big, deep, fluffy-lined pockets. In one of those huge, fluffy white pockets were my car keys!

Way to go, Karl!

Vernest Lange
Award Winning Photojournalist for
The New Jersey Star Ledger

In 2005 I had the pleasure of being introduced to Karl. I have many acquaintances, but a limited group of people I consider real friends. Over the ensuing years I have been a witness to Karl's prescient abilities. I have seen him spend countless hours helping people find solutions to a various array of problems. He has the unique ability to find answers that bring comfort and peace where previously there were only confusion and grief. The most amazing aspect of Karl, unlike so many who have been given certain gifts, is that he absolutely refuses any type of payment or recompense for his help.

I admire him for his unselfish dedication to many in need. With that being said, I never thought I would be one of them. In my darkest days, involving a death of a beloved pet, Karl was the one who saved me. He brought me out of a deep depression that was quite serious, and guided me through a horrific lawsuit involving a very minor dog bite. Without Karl's help, I truly do not know where I would be today. I certainly would not be the thriving individual I am.

Karl patiently listened and counseled me for over three years. He told me what the resolution to this unbelievable lawsuit would be, and that I really had nothing to worry about. Karl actually gave me the date of the resolution, and the settlement amount. Yes, he was 100 percent correct. But, most importantly, he counseled me and definitely helped me with my grief and guilt issues. What did he ask for all these years of aiding me? Only that we still remain friends. That will never change, nor will my eternal gratitude.

Jason Vigorito
Past Worshipful Master Adoniram Freemason Lodge,
Lyndhurst, New Jersey

My father and stepmother purchased a cape cod house in the northern New Jersey town of Hawthorne. After initially moving in, they began making renovations. They started with gutting the kitchen and dining room areas. Shortly after beginning these projects, my parents began to feel and sense that they were not their home's only occupants. My father eventually began to see a woman at the foot of their bed at night, and asked her repeatedly to leave, but she would just keep staring at my stepmother with intense silence. Knowing about Karl, my parents asked if he could pay a visit to the house and help them figure out the supernatural situation. Karl obliged, and I brought him over one evening. He asked everybody to stay quiet while he walked around the house. The last rooms Karl approached were the upstairs bedrooms, after which he came downstairs and explained to us the following:

There were two entities in the house, both of whom were centered in my parents' bedroom. The spirit that my father saw was my stepmother's grandmother, who was lingering out of maternal concerns for her. Karl assured her grandmother that all was well and fine with her granddaughter. There was a second entity as well: an elderly woman sitting in a rocking chair in the corner of the bedroom. She was a previous owner of the house, and she wanted to know what was going on with all the changes. Karl conveyed to her that it was my parents' house now, and they were upgrading it to modern standards and their personal tastes. The explanation satisfied the woman. Neither entity bothered my parents anymore after Karl's visit.

Follow Karl Petry on Facebook!
Go to https://www.facebook.com/karl.petry.3?fref=ts

Coming soon from Visionary Living Publishing, Karl's second book with more strange cases and investigations!